Transiti...   ...ore

enVisionMATH™

Authors

Randall I. Charles
Professor Emeritus
Department of Mathematics
San Jose State University
San Jose, California

Janet H. Caldwell
Professor of Mathematics
Rowan University
Glassboro, New Jersey

Mary Cavanagh
Executive Director of Center for Practice,
Research, and Innovation in Mathematics
Education (PRIME)
Arizona State University
Mesa, Arizona

Juanita Copley
Professor Emerita, College of Education
University of Houston
Houston, Texas

Warren Crown
Professor Emeritus of Mathematics Education
Graduate School of Education
Rutgers University
New Brunswick, New Jersey

Francis (Skip) Fennell
L. Stanley Bowlsbey Professor of Education
and Graduate and Professional Studies
McDaniel College
Westminster, Maryland

Stuart J. Murphy
Visual Learning Specialist
Boston, Massachusetts

Kay B. Sammons
Coordinator of Elementary Mathematics
Howard County Public Schools
Ellicott City, Maryland

Jane F. Schielack
Professor of Mathematics
Associate Dean for Assessment and
Pre K-12 Education, College of Science
Texas A&M University
College Station, Texas

William Tate
Edward Mallinckrodt Distinguished University
Professor in Arts & Sciences
Washington University
St. Louis, Missouri

Mathematicians

David M. Bressoud
DeWittWallace Professor of Mathematics
Macalester College
St. Paul, Minnesota

Roger Howe
Professor of Mathematics
Yale University
New Haven, Connecticut

Gary Lippman
Professor of Mathematics and Computer Science
California State University East Bay
Hayward, California

PEARSON

Glenview, Illinois • Boston, Massachusetts • Chandler, Arizona • Upper Saddle River, New Jersey

ELL Consultant

Jim Cummins
Professor
The University of Toronto
Toronto, Canada

**Common Core State
Standards Reviewers**

Elizabeth Baker
Mathematics Coordinator
Gilbert Public Schools
Gilbert, Arizona

Amy Barber
K-12 Math Coach
Peninsula School District ESC
Gig Harbor, Washington

Laura Cua
Teacher
Columbus City Schools
Columbus, Ohio

Wafa Deeb-Westervelt
Assistant Superintendent for
Curriculum, Instruction, and
Professional Development
Freeport Public Schools
Freeport, New York

Lynn Gullette
Title 1 Math Intervention
Mobile County Public Schools
Gilliard Elementary
Mobile, Alabama

Beverly K. Kimes
Director of Mathematics
Birmingham City Schools
Birmingham, Alabama

Kelly O'Rourke
Elementary School Assistant Principal
Clark County School District
Las Vegas, Nevada

Piper L. Riddle
Evidence-Based Learning Specialist
Canyons School District
Sandy, Utah

Debra L. Vitale
Math Coach
Bristol Public Schools
Bristol, Connecticut

Diane T. Wehby
Math Support Teacher
Birmingham City Schools
Birmingham, Alabama

Scott Foresman-Addison Wesley
enVisionMATH™

ISBN-13: 978-0-328-71552-7
ISBN-10: 0-328-71552-2

1 2 3 4 5 6 7 8 9 10 V011 15 14 13 12 11

Common Core
Student Lessons

Lesson 1-3A

Common Core

4.NBT.1 Recognize that in a multi-digit whole number, a digit in one place represents ten times what it represents in the place to its right. Also 4.NBT.2

Place Value Relationships

Hands-On place-value blocks

How are the digits in a multi-digit number related to each other?

Kiana collected 110 bottle caps. What is the relationship between the values of the digit 1 in each place?

110 bottle caps

Guided Practice

MATHEMATICAL PRACTICES

Do you know HOW?

In **1** through **2**, name the values of the given digits.

1. the 7s in 7,700

2. the 4s in 442

In **3** through **4**, what is the relationship between the values of the given digits?

3. the 7s in 7,700

4. the 4s in 442

Do you UNDERSTAND?

5. Reason Is the value of the first 4 ten times as great as the value of the second 4 in 4,043? Explain why or why not.

6. Reason Is the value of the 2 in 230 ten times as great as the value of the 3 in the same number? Explain why or why not.

Independent Practice

MATHEMATICAL PRACTICES

Look for Patterns In **7–22**, name the values of the given digits in the numbers below.

7. the 4s in 6,448   **8.** the 3s in 433   **9.** the 6s in 6,674   **10.** the 1s in 5,711

11. the 5s in 4,559   **12.** the 2s in 722   **13.** the 9s in 4,998   **14.** the 4s in 844

15. the 8s in 8,800   **16.** the 7s in 2,773   **17.** the 2s in 225   **18.** the 1s in 1,138

19. the 5s in 5,590   **20.** the 6s in 2,366   **21.** the 8s in 688   **22.** the 9s in 9,993

DIGITAL   eTools
www.pearsonsuccessnet.com

The first 1 is in the hundreds place. Its value is 100.

The second 1 is in the tens place. Its value is 10.

How is 100 related to 10?

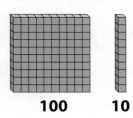

100   10

100 is ten times as much as 10. The first 1 is worth ten times as much as the second 1!

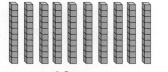

10 tens   1 ten

When two digits next to each other in a number are the same, the digit on the left is always ten times as great as the digit on the right.

Problem Solving

MATHEMATICAL
PRACTICES

23. Reason What can you say about the 3s in the number 43,335?

24. Critique Reasoning Mia says that in the number 5,555, all the digits have the same value. Is she correct? Explain why or why not.

25. Writing to Explain Sal says he is thinking of a 3-digit number in which all of the digits are the same. He says that the value of the digit in the tens place is 80. How can you find the value of the digit on the left and the right of the tens place?

26. Which of the following names the value of the 4s in the number 4,449?

A   4,000, 400, 40   C   4,000, 40, 4

B   4,000, 400, 4   D   400, 40, 4

27. The number 6,644 contains two sets of digits in which one digit is ten times as great as the other. Find the values of the digits in each set.

28. In the number 6,339, which places contain digits where one digit is ten times as great as the other?

29. In the number 7,882, if you move from the 8 in the hundreds place to the 8 in the tens place, what happens to the value of the 8?

30. Look for Patterns In the number 222, what is the relationship between the 2s? Think about the value of each 2 to help you find your answer.

31. Critique Reasoning Vin says that in the number 4,346, one 4 is 10 times as great as the other 4. Is he correct? Explain why or why not.

32. Describe the relationship between the values of the two 7s in the number 737.

Lesson 1-7A

Common Core

4.MD.2 Use the four operations to solve word problems involving distances, intervals of time, liquid volumes, masses of objects, and money, including problems involving simple fractions or decimals, and problems that require expressing measurements given in a larger unit in terms of a smaller unit. Represent measurement quantities using diagrams such as number line diagrams that feature a measurement scale.

Solving Problems Involving Money

How can you use counting up to make change?

How can you count to make change from a $20 bill used to buy the toy airplane?

 penny 1¢

 nickel 5¢

 dime 10¢

 quarter 25¢

 half dollar 50¢

 $8.36

Guided Practice

MATHEMATICAL PRACTICES

Do you know HOW?

For **1** and **2**, tell the amount of change for each situation.

1. You give the salesperson a $10 bill and three $5 bills to buy two movie tickets. How much change should you get?

MOVIE TICKET $11.25

2. A new jacket costs $65.89. How much change should you get if you give the salesperson four $20 bills?

Do you UNDERSTAND?

3. Reason In the example above, how could mental math be used to find the amount of change, rather than counting up with coins?

4. Reason If an item costs $19.54, why might someone give the sales clerk a $20 bill and 4 pennies?

Independent Practice

For **5–8**, tell the amount of change for each situation.

5. Andie buys a sandwich from the deli for $4.45. She pays for the sandwich with a $5 bill. How much change should she receive?

6. A new drawing pad costs $6.89. How much change should you get if you give the salesperson a $20 bill?

7. Carlos buys some knee pads and elbow pads. The total cost of the pads is $14.38. How much change should Carlos receive if he pays for the pads with two $10 bills?

8. Dana buys a poster that costs $8.15. She pays for the poster with a $10 dollar bill and one quarter. How much change should she receive?

4

One Way

Start with $8.36. Count up using the fewest coins.

Give this		Get this
4 pennies	→	$8.40
1 dime	→	$8.50
1 half dollar	→	$9
1 $1 bill	→	$10
1 $10 bill	→	$20

Another Way

Start with $8.36. Count up a different way.

Give this		Get this
4 pennies	→	$8.40
2 nickels	→	$8.50
2 quarters	→	$9
1 $1 bill	→	$10
2 $5 bills	→	$20

The change is the total amount given, $11.64.

Problem Solving

MATHEMATICAL PRACTICES

9. Reason Lucy buys a magazine for $4.19. She gives the sales clerk a $5 bill and two dimes. What is her change?

10. Marco used a $10 bill to pay for a jump rope. He received $3.08 in change. How much did the jump rope cost?

11. Reason Leo went to lunch with his parents. The bill was $17.85. What are two different combinations of coins and bills that can be used to make this amount?

12. Reason Leo's family used a $20 bill to pay the $17.85 lunch bill. What are three different combinations of coins and bills that can be used to make the change?

13. Blake bought two concert tickets for a total of $38.75. She gave the salesperson three $10 bills and two $5 bills. How much change should the salesperson give Blake?

14. Model Rajeev bought a skateboard that cost $37.74. How much change will he get back if he paid with two $20 bills?

    A $2.26   **C** $2.74

    B $3.26   **D** $3.74

15. Ana Maria wants to buy a sweater and a scarf that cost a total of $31.24. She has three $10 bills. How much more money does she need to buy both items?

16. Critique Reasoning Matthew buys a video game for $34.28. He pays for the game using two $20 bills. Matthew thinks he should receive $6.72 in change. Is he correct? Explain.

17. Communicate Jenna bought a hand pump for $12.19. She gave the sales clerk one $20 bill and one quarter. How can you find Jenna's change?

18. Greg buys three tickets. Each ticket costs $4.25. He pays for the tickets with three $5 bills. How much change should Greg get back?

Lesson 5-6A

Common Core

4.NBT.5 Multiply a whole number of up to four digits by a one-digit whole number, and multiply two two-digit numbers, using strategies based on place value and the properties of operations. Illustrate and explain the calculation by using equations, rectangular arrays, and/or area models. Also **4.OA.3**

Connecting the Expanded and Standard Algorithms

What is a common way to record multiplication?

A small school bus holds 24 passengers. A small jet holds 4 times as many passengers. How many passengers does the small jet hold?

Find 4×24.

? Passengers

Small jet | 24 | 24 | 24 | 24 | ← 4 times as many

School bus | 24

Guided Practice

MATHEMATICAL PRACTICES

Do you know HOW?

In **1** through **6**, find each product two ways. First use the expanded algorithm, and then use the standard algorithm.

1. 5×17 **2.** 3×43

3. 4×56 **4.** 6×62

5. $\begin{array}{r} 29 \\ \times\ 3 \\ \hline \end{array}$ **6.** $\begin{array}{r} 88 \\ \times\ 2 \\ \hline \end{array}$

Do you UNDERSTAND?

7. Critique Reasoning Mara used the expanded algorithm shown to the right. Is she correct? Explain.

$\begin{array}{r} 24 \\ \times\ 4 \\ \hline 80 \\ +\ 16 \\ \hline 96 \end{array}$

8. A ferry can carry 16 cars. How many cars can the ferry carry in 5 trips?

Independent Practice

In **9** through **24**, find each product. Use either method.

9. 6×38 **10.** 4×47 **11.** 8×42 **12.** 5×64

13. 7×26 **14.** 9×33 **15.** 2×76 **16.** 4×29

17. $\begin{array}{r} 17 \\ \times\ 9 \\ \hline \end{array}$ **18.** $\begin{array}{r} 61 \\ \times\ 3 \\ \hline \end{array}$ **19.** $\begin{array}{r} 45 \\ \times\ 7 \\ \hline \end{array}$ **20.** $\begin{array}{r} 83 \\ \times\ 5 \\ \hline \end{array}$

21. $\begin{array}{r} 23 \\ \times\ 5 \\ \hline \end{array}$ **22.** $\begin{array}{r} 18 \\ \times\ 8 \\ \hline \end{array}$ **23.** $\begin{array}{r} 53 \\ \times\ 3 \\ \hline \end{array}$ **24.** $\begin{array}{r} 37 \\ \times\ 7 \\ \hline \end{array}$

6

One Way

Expanded Algorithm

Find the partial products.

```
   24
 ×  4
  ───
   16  ←─── Partial
 + 80  ←─── Products
  ───
   96
```

The jet can hold 96 passengers.

Another Way

Standard Algorithm

First, multiply the ones. Regroup if needed.

```
   1
  24      4 × 4 ones = 16 ones
 ×  4     Regroup 16 ones
 ───      as 1 ten 6 ones.
    6
```

Then, multiply the tens. Add any extra tens.

```
   1
  24      4 × 2 tens = 8 tens
 ×  4     There is 1 extra ten.
 ───      8 tens + 1 ten = 9 tens
   96
```

The jet can hold 96 passengers.

Problem Solving

 **MATHEMATICAL PRACTICES**

25. A speedboat holds 12 adults and 6 children. How many people in all can go on 4 speedboat rides?

© 26. Look for Patterns Vera created a design using 68 tiles. If she doubles her design and then doubles it again, how many tiles will she use in all?

© 27. Estimation In 2008, a surfer set a world record for stand up paddle surfing. In 24 hours, he paddled 49 miles. About how far did he go each hour?

28. Luis recycles aluminum cans. His goal was to recycle 10,000 cans by May 1. He recycled 3,789 cans in March and 5,068 cans in April. How many cans is Luis over or under his goal? Explain how you found your answer.

29. 🌐 **Social Studies** In the Aztec calendar, each year has a number from 1 to 13. It also has one of four signs: house, rabbit, reed, or flint. It takes 4 × 13 years to go through one complete cycle of years. How many years are in one cycle?

30. Belle used 286 pages of newspaper to make a volcano of papier-mâché. What is this number rounded to the nearest hundred?

    A 200   **C** 290

    B 280   **D** 300

31. 🔎 **Science** Eucalyptus trees grow in Southern Florida. How much taller would a fast-growing eucalyptus tree be after 7 years?

A fast-growing eucalyptus can grow about 11 feet each year.

Lesson
5-8A

© **Common Core**

4.NBT.5 Multiply a whole number of up to four digits by a one-digit whole number, and multiply two two-digit numbers, using strategies based on place value and the properties of operations. Illustrate and explain the calculation by using equations, rectangular arrays, and/or area models.

Multiplying 3- and 4-Digit by 1-Digit Numbers

How do you multiply larger numbers?

Juan guessed that the large bottle had 3 times as many pennies as the small bottle. What was Juan's guess?

Choose an Operation Multiply to find "3 times as many."

264 pennies

Other Examples

Find 3 × 2,746.

Step 1	**Step 2**	**Step 3**	**Step 4**
Multiply the ones. Regroup if necessary.	Multiply the tens. Add any extra tens. Regroup if necessary.	Multiply the hundreds. Add any extra hundreds. Regroup if necessary.	Multiply the thousands. Add any extra thousands. Regroup if necessary.

$$
\begin{array}{r}
\overset{1}{2,746} \\
\times\quad 3 \\
\hline
8
\end{array}
\qquad
\begin{array}{r}
\overset{1\,1}{2,746} \\
\times\quad 3 \\
\hline
38
\end{array}
\qquad
\begin{array}{r}
\overset{2\,1\,1}{2,746} \\
\times\quad 3 \\
\hline
238
\end{array}
\qquad
\begin{array}{r}
\overset{2\,1\,1}{2,746} \\
\times\quad 3 \\
\hline
8,238
\end{array}
$$

Find 5 × 3,138

Step 1	**Step 2**	**Step 3**	**Step 4**
Multiply the ones. Regroup if necessary.	Multiply the tens. Add any extra tens. Regroup if necessary.	Multiply the hundreds. Add any extra hundreds. Regroup if necessary.	Multiply the thousands. Add any extra thousands. Regroup if necessary.

$$
\begin{array}{r}
\overset{4}{3,138} \\
\times\quad 5 \\
\hline
0
\end{array}
\qquad
\begin{array}{r}
\overset{1\,4}{3,138} \\
\times\quad 5 \\
\hline
90
\end{array}
\qquad
\begin{array}{r}
\overset{1\,4}{3,138} \\
\times\quad 5 \\
\hline
690
\end{array}
\qquad
\begin{array}{r}
\overset{1\,4}{3,138} \\
\times\quad 5 \\
\hline
15,690
\end{array}
$$

Guided Practice

 MATHEMATICAL PRACTICES

Do you know HOW?

In **1** and **2**, find each product. Estimate to check for reasonableness.

1. $\begin{array}{r} 519 \\ \times\quad 4 \\ \hline \end{array}$

2. $\begin{array}{r} 3,378 \\ \times\quad 2 \\ \hline \end{array}$

Do you UNDERSTAND?

© **3. Reason** In the example at the top, 3 × 6 tens is how many tens?

4. A band performed 4 sold-out shows. All 2,428 seats were filled for each show. How many fans saw the 4 shows?

Step 1	Step 2	Step 3

Step 1

Multiply the ones. Regroup if needed.

$$\begin{array}{r} ^1 \\ 264 \\ \times \quad 3 \\ \hline 2 \end{array}$$

3 × 4 ones = 12 ones or 1 ten 2 ones

Step 2

Multiply the tens. Add any extra tens. Regroup if needed.

$$\begin{array}{r} ^{1\,1} \\ 264 \\ \times \quad 3 \\ \hline 92 \end{array}$$

(3 × 6 tens) + 1 ten = 19 tens or 1 hundred 9 tens

Step 3

Multiply the hundreds. Add any extra hundreds.

$$\begin{array}{r} ^{1\,1} \\ 264 \\ \times \quad 3 \\ \hline 792 \end{array}$$

(3 × 2 hundreds) + 1 hundred = 7 hundreds

Juan's guess was 792 pennies.

Independent Practice

In **5** through **12**, find each product. Estimate to check reasonableness.

5. $\begin{array}{r} 423 \\ \times \quad 2 \\ \hline \end{array}$
6. $\begin{array}{r} 3,942 \\ \times \quad 4 \\ \hline \end{array}$
7. $\begin{array}{r} 6,271 \\ \times \quad 3 \\ \hline \end{array}$
8. $\begin{array}{r} 159 \\ \times \quad 5 \\ \hline \end{array}$

9. 2 × 125
10. 3 × 3,196
11. 4 × 265
12. 5 × 4,129

Problem Solving

MATHEMATICAL PRACTICES

Ⓒ **Reason** In **13** through **15**, use the information in the pictures below to find the weight of each animal.

13. Horse **14.** Rhino **15.** Elephant

Bear: Weighs 836 pounds

Horse: Weighs 2 times as much as the bear

Rhino: Weighs 5 times as much as the bear

Elephant: Weighs 9 times as much as the bear

Use the table at the right for **16** through **21**.

Electronics Sale	
Mobile Phone	$135
Digital Camera	$295
Laptop Computer	$1,075
Flat-Screen TV	$1,650

16. **Estimation** About how much did Dr. Sims spend if he bought 3 flat-screen TVs for his office?

17. **Persevere** Which costs more—2 laptop computers or 4 digital cameras? Use number sense to decide.

18. **Model** Which tells how to find the total cost of a laptop computer and 5 digital cameras?

   A 5 × $295 × $1,075

   B $1,075 + (5 × $295)

   C $1,075 + $295

   D $295 + (5 × $1,075)

19. Larry is saving money to buy 2 mobile phones and a laptop computer. How much additional money will he need to save if he has already saved $400?

   A $675   **C** $945

   B $810   **D** $1,345

20. What did Mr. Sims buy at the electronics sale if (3 × $295) + $1,075 stands for the total price?

21. Mrs. Lee goes to the electronic sale with $3,275. Does she have enough money to buy 2 flat-screen TV's? Why or why not?

22. **Social Studies** The Appalachian Trail is 2,174 miles long. If Andy hiked the entire trail one time, how many miles did he hike?

   A 1 mile

   B 1,087 miles

   C 2,174 miles

   D 4,348 miles

23. If Chuck's Sports sold 124 fishing poles each month, how many fishing poles would be sold in four months?

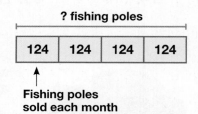

? fishing poles

| 124 | 124 | 124 | 124 |

Fishing poles
sold each month

24. Renting a boat at a marina costs $118 a day. If the marina rented 8 boats in one day, how much money was earned from the rentals?

25. A manager at a fast food restaurant orders 8 packages of napkins. Each package contains 375 napkins. How many napkins did the manager order?

Find each product. Estimate to check
if the answer is reasonable.

1. 21	**2.** 843	**3.** 6,318	**4.** 528
× 4	× 6	× 5	× 9

5. 40	**6.** 17	**7.** 2,175	**8.** 796
× 3	× 8	× 2	× 7

9. 4,927	**10.** 1,234	**11.** 700	**12.** 99	**13.** 5,364
× 6	× 9	× 5	× 9	× 4

Find each difference. Estimate to check
if the answer is reasonable.

14. 3,427 − 648　　　**15.** 7,005 − 6,496　　　**16.** 502 − 89

Error Search Find each product that is not correct.
Write it correctly and explain the error.

17. 6,829	**18.** 438	**19.** 2,365	**20.** 45	**21.** 777
× 5	× 9	× 3	× 4	× 7
34,145	3,872	7,098	49	5,439

Number Sense

Estimating and Reasoning Write whether each
statement is true or false. Explain your answer.

22. The product of 6 and 39 is less than 240.

23. The sum of 3,721 and 1,273 is greater than 4,000 but less than 6,000.

24. The product of 5 and 286 is greater than 1,500.

25. The product of 4 and 3,123 is closer to 12,000 than 16,000.

26. The sum of 4,637 and 2,878 is greater than 8,000.

27. The quotient of 4 divided by 1 is 1.

4.NBT.5 Multiply a whole number of up to four digits by a one-digit whole number, and multiply two two-digit numbers, using strategies based on place value and the properties of operations. Illustrate and explain the calculation by using equations, rectangular arrays, and/or area models.

Arrays and an Expanded Algorithm

How can you record multiplication?

Marcia picked oranges and put them in 12 mesh bags. Each bag had the same number of oranges. What is the total number of oranges Marcia picked?

Choose an Operation
Multiply to join equal groups.

15 oranges in each bag

Guided Practice

© MATHEMATICAL **PRACTICES**

Do you know HOW?

In **1** and **2**, find all the partial products. Then add to find the product.

1.   23
     × 14

2.   41
     × 25

Do you UNDERSTAND?

3. In the example above, why do you find 2 × 10 rather than 2 × 1?

© **4. Writing to Explain** Could you record the four partial products in the example above in a different order? Explain.

Independent Practice

Leveled Practice In **5** through **8**, find all the partial products. Then add to find the product.

5.   34
     × 51

6.   73
     × 81

7.   64
     × 32

8.   26
     × 53

In **9** through **16**, use the expanded algorithm to find each product.

9. 18 × 19

10. 42 × 16

11. 15 × 64

12. 27 × 51

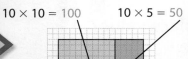

Find 12 × 15.
Use an array to model 12 × 15.

10 × 10 = 100   10 × 5 = 50

2 × 10 = 20   2 × 5 = 10

Step 1

Use the expanded algorithm to find 12 × 15.
Multiply the ones.

$$
\begin{array}{r}
15 \\
\times\ 12 \\
\hline
10 \quad 2 \times 5 = 10 \\
20 \quad 2 \times 10 = 20 \\
\end{array}
$$

10 and 20 are partial products.

Step 2

Multiply the tens. Then add all the partial products.

$$
\begin{array}{r}
15 \\
\times\ 12 \\
\hline
10 \\
20 \\
50 \quad 10 \times 5 = 50 \\
+\ 100 \quad 10 \times 10 = 100 \\
\hline
180 \\
\end{array}
$$

Marcia picked 180 oranges.

13. 17 × 38 **14.** 33 × 24 **15.** 43 × 19 **16.** 52 × 23

Problem Solving

Ⓒ **17. Reason** A pair of one type of shoes weighs 15 ounces. The shoebox they come in weighs 2 ounces. Which is the total weight of 15 pairs of these shoes, including the boxes?

A   147 ounces   C   225 ounces

B   155 ounces   D   255 ounces

18. A surveyor measures the length of two runways at an airport. The first runway, Runway 9, is 13,000 feet long. The second runway, Runway 12, is 9,354 feet long. How much shorter is Runway 12 than Runway 9?

Ⓒ **19. Estimation** Sara estimated 23 × 43 by using 20 × 40. Sam estimated 23 × 43 by using 25 × 40. Explain why Sam's method will give a closer estimate than Sara's method.

Ⓒ **20. Construct Arguments** A school has two large patios. One is rectangular and is 24 feet long by 18 feet wide. The other is square and each side is 21 feet long. Which patio has a greater perimeter? Explain.

21. The Castillo de San Marcos is a Spanish fortress that was built between 1672 and 1695. Rounded to the nearest ten thousand, how many pesos did it cost to build the fortress at that time?

It cost 138,375 pesos to build this fortress.

© Common Core

4.NBT.6 Find whole-number quotients and remainders with up to four-digit dividends and one-digit divisors, using strategies based on place value, the properties of operations, and/or the relationship between multiplication and division. Illustrate and explain the calculation by using equations, rectangular arrays, and/or area models. Also **4.OA.3**

Estimating Quotients for Greater Dividends

How do you estimate quotients using place value?

On a "Clean Up Your Town Day," 1,320 people volunteered to clean up the Springville parks. They were divided equally into teams to work in each of the town's parks. About how many people were in each team?

Springville's parks

Guided Practice

© MATHEMATICAL PRACTICES

Do you know HOW?

In **1** through **6**, use multiplication facts to help estimate each quotient.

1. 3,340 ÷ 8   **2.** 2,943 ÷ 7

3. 552 ÷ 9   **4.** 776 ÷ 4

5. 2,013 ÷ 5   **6.** 281 ÷ 3

Do you UNDERSTAND?

© **7. Reason** What multiplication fact could you use to estimate the quotient 2,000 ÷ 4? How is this problem different from the others in this lesson?

8. When dividing a 4-digit number by a 1-digit number, how many digits can the quotient have?

Independent Practice

In **9** through **28**, estimate each quotient.

 Tip *For numbers greater than 1,000, round to the nearest hundred. Then try multiples of one hundred that are near the rounded dividend.*

9. 497 ÷ 8   **10.** 4,971 ÷ 8   **11.** 3,051 ÷ 7   **12.** 305 ÷ 7

13. 779 ÷ 7   **14.** 7,779 ÷ 7   **15.** 3,688 ÷ 6   **16.** 423 ÷ 4

17. 5,684 ÷ 9   **18.** 5,346 ÷ 6   **19.** 508 ÷ 7   **20.** 2,120 ÷ 5

21. 647 ÷ 3   **22.** 3,958 ÷ 8   **23.** 224 ÷ 3   **24.** 915 ÷ 3

25. 279 ÷ 9   **26.** 2,449 ÷ 8   **27.** 3,124 ÷ 6   **28.** 4,519 ÷ 5

One Way

Use multiplication patterns.

6 times what number is about 1,320?

I know $6 \times 2 = 12$, so
$$6 \times 20 = 120 \text{ and}$$
$$6 \times 200 = 1,200.$$

1,200 is close enough to 1,320 for this estimate.

Another Way

Use estimation and division facts.

Estimate the quotient $1,320 \div 6$.

$$12 \div 6 = 2$$
$$120 \div 6 = 20$$
$$1,200 \div 6 = 200$$

$1,320 \div 6$ is about 200. Each team is made up of about 200 people.

Problem Solving

 MATHEMATICAL PRACTICES

In **29** through **34**, estimate each quotient.

29. In 1999, an 89-year-old woman walked 3,055 miles across the United States. She walked about 9 miles each day. About how many days did it take her to walk across the United States?

30. Casey is reading a book that has 169 pages. He reads about 9 pages a day. About how many days will it take for him to finish the book?

31. Reason The students who run the school store ordered 1,440 pencils. They are putting them in packages of 6 pencils. About how many packages can they make? Will the exact answer be more or less than the estimate?

32. Ramon's older sister wants to buy a car that costs $7,993. She earns $9 for every hour she works. About how many hours must she work to earn enough money to buy the car?

  A 80 hours   **C** 800 hours

  B 90 hours   **D** 900 hours

33. Reasonableness Eight students can fit at one cafeteria table. About how many tables are needed for 231 students? Does your answer make sense? How can you tell?

34. Persevere Laura's dog eats 1 bag of dog food every 6 days. About how many bags will he eat in 1 year?

  Tip *1 year = 365 days*

35. Writing to Explain What is the first step when you estimate the answer to a division problem?

36. Andrea rides her bike 16 miles each week. How many miles will she ride her bike in 39 weeks?

Lesson
8-3B
©
Common
Core

4.NBT.6 Find whole-number quotients and remainders with up to four-digit dividends and one-digit divisors, using strategies based on place value, the properties of operations, and/or the relationship between multiplication and division. Illustrate and explain the calculation by using equations, rectangular arrays, and/or area models.

Using Objects to Divide: Division as Repeated Subtraction

How can subtraction help you divide?

Su has 24 international postage stamps. She needs 2 of these stamps to send a postcard. How many postcards can she send using all of these stamps?

24 stamps

Think How many 2s are in 24?

Guided Practice

© MATHEMATICAL PRACTICES

Do you know HOW?

Use counters and repeated subtraction to divide. Record your work.

1. How many 3s are in 48?

2. How many 4s are in 60?

Do you UNDERSTAND?

© **3. Writing to Explain** Explain the shortcut this student used for solving the postcard problem above.

$24 - 10 = 14$ (5 groups of 2)
$14 - 10 = 4$ (5 more groups of 2)
 $4 - 4 = 0$ (2 more groups of 2)

12 postcards

Independent Practice

For **4** through **17** use counters and repeated subtraction to divide. Record your work.

4. How many 5s are in 35?

5. How many 4s are in 32?

6. How many 7s are in 84?

7. How many 6s are in 66?

8. How many 8s are in 72?

9. How many 3s are in 57?

10. $56 \div 7$

11. $54 \div 9$

12. $30 \div 2$

13. $84 \div 6$

14. $80 \div 5$

15. $112 \div 8$

16. $88 \div 8$

17. $117 \div 9$

Use counters to model 24 stamps. Take away 2 as many times as possible.

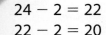

Take away 2.

Take away 2.

24 − 2 = 22
22 − 2 = 20

Continue to take away 2 as many times as possible. Record using symbols.

20 − 2 = 18	10 − 2 = 8
18 − 2 = 16	8 − 2 = 6
16 − 2 = 14	6 − 2 = 4
14 − 2 = 12	4 − 2 = 2
12 − 2 = 10	2 − 2 = 0

Since 2 was subtracted 12 times, Su can send 12 postcards.

Problem Solving

18. Teams of 4 students will be formed for a scavenger hunt. How many teams will be formed if 52 students signed up?

19. Mary wants to share her collection of 42 marbles equally among 3 of her friends. How many marbles will each of her friends receive?

20. Billy is organizing his football cards into 3 equal stacks. How many cards should he put in each stack if he has a total of 75 football cards?

   A 15   **C** 25

   B 20   **D** 40

21. A pizza is cut into 12 pieces for 4 people to share equally. How many pieces will each person receive?

   A 3   **C** 1

   B 2   **D** 0

© **22. Critique Reasoning** Paul claims that when he organizes his collection of 70 marbles into 5 equal piles that there will be 15 marbles in each pile. Is Paul correct? Why or why not?

70 marbles in all

23. The 240 students at Cypress Elementary are taking a field trip. How many vans are needed to transport the students, if each van will hold 8 students?

24. Jeff buys a box of 30 apples. He eats 2 apples each day at lunch. How long will the apples last?

4.NBT.6 Find whole-number quotients and remainders with up to four-digit dividends and one-digit divisors, using strategies based on place value, the properties of operations, and/or the relationship between multiplication and division. Illustrate and explain the calculation by using equations, rectangular arrays, and/or area models.

Division as Repeated Subtraction

How can you record division using repeated subtraction?

Each row on an airplane can seat 3 people. If there are 63 people waiting in line and each seat will be taken, how many rows of seats are needed?

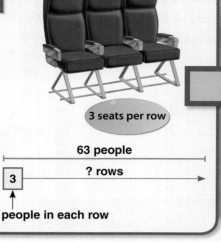

3 seats per row

Think How many 3s are in 63?

Guided Practice

MATHEMATICAL
PRACTICES

Do you know HOW?

Use repeated subtraction to divide. Record your work.

1. 48 ÷ 4

2. 75 ÷ 5

3. 153 ÷ 9

4. 65 ÷ 5

Do you UNDERSTAND?

Use repeated subtraction to divide. Record your work.

5. Reason Show one way of using repeated subtraction to solve. 69 ÷ 3.

6. Reason Show another way of using repeated subtraction to solve. 69 ÷ 3.

Independent Practice

For **7** through **14** use repeated subtraction to divide. Record your work.

7. 78 ÷ 6   **8.** 84 ÷ 7   **9.** 88 ÷ 8   **10.** 42 ÷ 3

11. 90 ÷ 6   **12.** 40 ÷ 2   **13.** 92 ÷ 4   **14.** 126 ÷ 7

Problem Solving

MATHEMATICAL
PRACTICES

15. There are 5 players on a basketball team. How many teams can be formed from a list of 90 players?

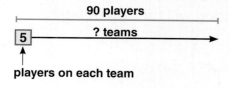

16. A collection of 64 stickers is being placed into 4 equal piles. How many stickers will be placed in each pile?

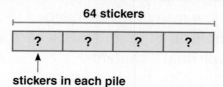

Here is one way to record the division problem 63 ÷ 3.

63   Estimate: How many 3s are in 63? Try 10.
−30 Multiply 10 × 3 and subtract.
33   Estimate: How many 3s are in 33? Use 11.
−33 Multiply 11 × 3 and subtract.
0

10 + 11 = 21, so there are 21 3s in 63.

21 rows are needed to seat 63 people.

Here is another way to record the division problem.

63   Estimate: How many 3s are in 63? Try 20.
−60 Multiply 20 × 3 and subtract.
3   Estimate: How many 3s are in 3? Use 1.
−3   Multiply 1 × 3 and subtract.
0

20 + 1 = 21, so there are 21 3s in 63.

21 rows are needed to seat 63 people.

17. Which statement below is the best estimate for the quotient 99 ÷ 3?

A between 0 and 10

B between 10 and 20

C between 20 and 30

D between 30 and 40

18. There are 2 dozen eggs in the kitchen. A chef is baking cookies for 3 birthday parties. For each party, the chef is using an equal number of eggs. How many eggs does the chef use for one party?

Tip *12 eggs = 1 dozen*

19. Critique Reasoning Amanda thinks that she can separate her books into 7 equal piles. Amanda has a total of 42 books. Is Amanda's reasoning correct?

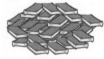

42 books

20. A photo album can hold 84 pictures. If 4 pictures are on each page, then how many pages are in the photo album?

A 25   **C** 20

B 21   **D** 16

21. Construct Arguments Ryan has a total of 85 pennies. Will he be able to give away his pennies equally to 4 of his friends? Explain your reasoning.

22. A local baker made 132 bagels one day. The baker sells bagels in packages of 6 bagels. He sold all of the bagels. How many packages of bagels did he sell?

23. Communicate How can you use repeated subtraction to divide 81 ÷ 3? Solve and explain your process.

24. A shoe store got a delivery of 104 pairs of shoes. There are 8 pairs of shoes in each case that was delivered. How many cases were delivered?

Lesson
8-8A

© Common Core

4.NBT.6 Find whole-number quotients and remainders with up to four-digit dividends and one-digit divisors, using strategies based on place value, the properties of operations, and/or the relationship between multiplication and division. Illustrate and explain the calculation by using equations, rectangular arrays, and/or area models.

Dividing 4-Digit by 1-Digit Numbers

How can you estimate larger quotients?

In all, 4,729 hot dogs were sold at a football game. If there are 8 hot dogs in a package, how many packages of hot dogs were sold?

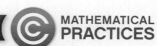

4,729 hot dogs sold

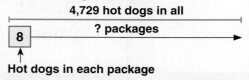

4,729 hot dogs in all

8   ? packages

Hot dogs in each package

Guided Practice

© **MATHEMATICAL PRACTICES**

Do you know HOW?

Divide. Start by estimating.

1. $9\overline{)2,871}$

2. $4\overline{)2,486}$

3. $9\overline{)691}$

4. $4\overline{)1,140}$

Do you UNDERSTAND?

© 5. **Reason** In the example above, how many hot dogs were left over in the extra package?

© 6. **Writing to Explain** Vickie's estimated quotient was 80. The actual quotient she calculated was 48. Is her actual quotient reasonable? Explain.

Independent Practice

Divide. Start by estimating.

7. $8\overline{)3,248}$

8. $5\overline{)247}$

9. $6\overline{)1,380}$

10. $5\overline{)3,980}$

In **11** through **16**, estimate first. Tell if the answers are reasonable. If the answer is not reasonable, find the correct answer.

11. $\overset{61 \text{ R}1}{6\overline{)367}}$

12. $\overset{911 \text{ R}6}{3\overline{)3,582}}$

13. $\overset{49 \text{ R}2}{5\overline{)247}}$

14. $\overset{93 \text{ R}8}{9\overline{)1,745}}$

15. $\overset{53 \text{ R}4}{7\overline{)375}}$

16. $\overset{91 \text{ R}7}{8\overline{)1,535}}$

Estimate. Decide where to start.	Divide.

Estimate. Decide where to start.

$$500 \times 8 = 4{,}000$$

The answer is more than 500.

$$600 \times 8 = 4{,}800$$

The answer is less than but close to 600.

Start dividing in the hundreds.

Divide.

```
      591 R1
8)4,729      47 hundreds ÷ 8 is about 5 hundreds
  -40        8 × 5 = 40
   72        72 tens ÷ 8 is 9 tens
  -72        8 × 9 = 72
   09        9 ones ÷ 8 is about 1 one
  - 8        8 × 1 = 8
    1
```

591 complete packages were sold and 1 hot dog was sold from another package.

Problem Solving

MATHEMATICAL
PRACTICES

Solve. Record your work.

17. A family of four drove from San Francisco to New York. They drove the same number of miles each day for 6 days. How many miles did they drive each day? What does the remainder mean?

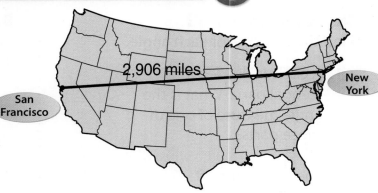

2,906 miles

San Francisco

New York

© 18. Reason Without dividing, how can you tell that the quotient for 5,873 ÷ 8 is greater than 700? Is the quotient less than 800? Explain.

© 19. Reason Chose a value for x so that $x \div 5$ is between 400 and 500. Tell how you decided.

20. ♪ **Music** A square dance set is made up of 4 couples (8 dancers). Each couple stands on one of the four sides of a square. There are 150 people at a square dance. What is the greatest number of sets possible at the dance?

    A 18   **B** 19   **C** 37   **D** 38

21. Michelle traveled 498 miles from Lakeside to West Little River. She made 7 stops along the way. Michelle estimated that she drove about 50 miles between stops. Is her estimate reasonable? Explain.

22. Mr. Girard sells fishing supplies. He traveled 527 miles from Jacksonville to Miami. He made 6 stops at equal intervals, including his final stop. About how many miles did he travel between stops?

23. Alycia has 164 treats to give to the 7 goats at the petting zoo. Each goat gets an equal share of the treats. How many treats will each goat get? How many treats will Alycia have left?

4.MD.5a An angle is measured with reference to a circle with its center at the common endpoint of the rays, by considering the fraction of the circular arc between the points where the two rays intersect the circle. An angle that turns through 1/360 of a circle is called a "one-degree angle," and can be used to measure angles. Also **4.MD.5, 4.G.1**

Understanding Angles and Unit Angles

What is the unit used to measure angles?

Jill drew a right angle and wants to find its measurement. Angles can be measured in units called degrees (°). A unit angle is an angle that cuts off $\frac{1}{360}$ of a circle and measures 1°. When you find the degrees of an angle, you find its angle measure.

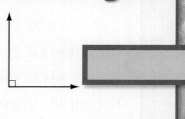

$1° = \frac{1}{360}$ of a circle

Guided Practice

© **MATHEMATICAL PRACTICES**

Do you know HOW?

Find the measure of each angle.

1. A circle is divided into 9 equal parts. What is the angle measure of one of those parts?

2. The angle cuts off $\frac{1}{8}$ of the circle.

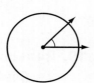

Do you UNDERSTAND?

© 3. **Critique Reasoning** Susan thinks Angle B is greater than Angle A? Do you agree? Explain.

4. Mike cuts a pie into 6 equal pieces. What is the angle measure of each piece? Explain.

Independent Practice

© **MATHEMATICAL PRACTICES**

© **Use Structure** For **5** through **12**, find the measure of each angle.

5. The angle cuts off $\frac{1}{5}$ of the circle.

6. The angle cuts off $\frac{3}{8}$ of the circle.

7.

8.

9.

10.

11. A circle is divided into 20 equal parts. Find the angle measure of one of the parts.

12. Find the measure of an angle that cuts off $\frac{3}{10}$ of a circle.

Animated Glossary
www.pearsonsuccessnet.com

Divide to find the angle measure of a right angle.

Right angles divide a circle into 4 equal parts.

$$360° \div 4 = 90°$$

The angle measure of a right angle is 90°.

What is the angle measure of a straight angle?

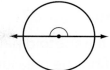

A straight angle divides a circle into 2 equal parts.

$$360° \div 2 = 180°$$

The angle measure of a straight angle is 180°.

Find the measure of an angle that cuts off $\frac{1}{6}$ of a circle.

Remember, $\frac{1}{6}$ means 1 of 6 equal parts, so divide by 6 to find the angle measure.

$$360° \div 6 = 60°$$

The angle measure is 60°.

Problem Solving

MATHEMATICAL
PRACTICES

For **13** through **21**, solve each problem.

13. Lanie cut a large circular rice cake into 3 pieces with equal angles. What is the angle measure of each piece?

14. What is the measure of the smaller angle when it is 8:00?

15. Megan has a very large round table. In order for her to seat her guests, she divided it into 15 equal sections. What is the angle measure of each section of the table?

ⓒ **16. Reason** Joanne cut a round pizza into equal wedges with angles measuring 36°. How many pieces of pizza does she have?

ⓒ **17. Construct Arguments** Jacey wrote an equation to find an angle measure. What do *a* and *b* stand for in Jacey's equation?

$$360 \div a = b$$

ⓒ **18. Writing to Explain** Why is 360 used as the dividend when dividing to find the measure of an angle?

19. Four pieces of pie were eaten from a pie cut in equal parts. The 5 pieces that remained measured 200°. What was the angle measure of one piece of pie?

ⓒ **20. Persevere** Jake cut a round gelatin dessert into 8 equal pieces. Five of the pieces were eaten. What angle measure of the dessert was left?

21. Estimation Paul drew a clock face that showed the time 5:00. What is the measure of the smaller angle shown by that time?

    A 50°   **B** 120°   **C** 135°   **D** 150°

Lesson
9-3B

Common
Core

4.MD.5b An angle that
turns through *n* one-degree
angles is said to have an
angle measure of *n* degrees.
Also 4.MD.5, 4.MD.5.a, 4.G.1

Measuring with Unit Angles

How are angles measured?

Holly traced around a trapezoid pattern block. She wants to find the measure of the angle formed at the vertex shown at the right. What can Holly use to measure the angle?

Hands-On
pattern blocks

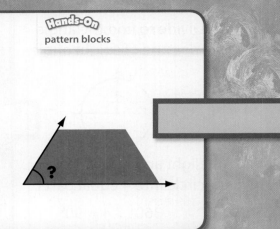

Guided Practice

MATHEMATICAL PRACTICES

Do you know HOW?

Use angles you know to find the measure of each angle. Explain how to use the measures of the angles in the squares to help.

1.   **Tip** *The corners of a square form 90° angles.*

2.

Do you UNDERSTAND?

3. **Communicate** Explain how you could draw a 210° angle.

4. How many 30° angles are there in a 180° angle? How do know?

5. How many 45° angles are there in a 180° angle? How do you know?

Independent Practice

MATHEMATICAL PRACTICES

Use Tools For **6** through **14**, find the measure of each angle. Use pattern blocks to help.

6.

7.

8.

9.

10.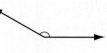

11.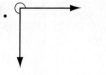

12.

13.

14.

DIGITAL
eTools
www.pearsonsuccessnet.com

Use an angle you know to find the measure of another angle.

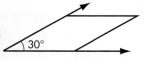

The smaller angle of this pattern block measures 30°.

It turns through 30 unit angles of 1°.

The smaller angle of the trapezoid pattern block matches two of the smaller angles on the long rhombus pattern block. Each smaller angle is 30°.

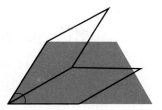

$2 \times 30° = 60°$

The measure of the angle is 60°.

Problem Solving

For **15** through **22,** solve each problem. Use pattern blocks to help.

15. What is the measure of each angle of the yellow hexagon pattern block?

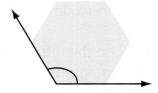

16. What is the measure of the smaller angle formed at 5:00?

17. Cory cut a pizza into 45° slices. Five of the slices were eaten. What is the angle measure of the pizza that is left?

18. What is the measure of the two different-sized angles of the blue rhombus pattern block?

© **19. Be Precise** A classroom table top is shaped like a trapezoid but with different pairs of angles than the red pattern block. What are the angle measures formed on the inside of the classroom table?

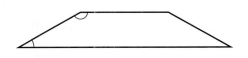

20. Using pattern blocks, what is the measure of the larger angle formed at 8:00?

   A 60°   **C** 175°

   B 120°   **D** 240°

© **21. Writing to Explain** How can you use pattern blocks to measure or draw an angle of 150°?

22. Critique Reasoning Jared said that the angle formed to show the time 10:00 is a 45° angle. Is he correct? Explain.

Lesson
9-4A

Common
Core

4.MD.7 Recognize angle measure as additive. When an angle is decomposed into non-overlapping parts, the angle measure of the whole is the sum of the angle measures of the parts. Solve addition and subtraction problems to find unknown angles ... by using an equation .... Also 4.MD.5.a, 4.MD.5.b, 4.MD.6

Adding and Subtracting Angle Measures

Hands-On
protractors

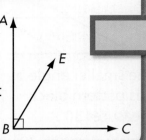

How can you add and subtract to find unknown angle measures?

Elinor is creating a design. First she draws a right angle, ∠ABC. Then she draws a ray BE. She finds that ∠EBC measures 60°. How can she find the measure of ∠ABE without using a protractor?

Guided Practice

MATHEMATICAL
PRACTICES

Do you know HOW?

For **1 and 2**, use the diagram next to each exercise. Add or subtract to find the angle measure.

1. What is the measure of ∠EBC if ∠ABE measures 25°?

2. What is the measure of ∠AEB if measures ∠CEB is 68°?

Do you UNDERSTAND?

ⓒ 3. **Use Structure** Write the equation you used to find the answer to Exercise **2**. What is another way to write it using a different operation?

ⓒ 4. **Model** Use the information below to draw a diagram.
   ∠PQR measures 42°.
   ∠RQS measures 39°.
   ∠PQR and ∠RQS do not overlap.
   What is the measure of ∠PQS?

Independent Practice

For **5 and 6**, use the diagram at the right.

5. What is the measure of ∠FGJ if ∠JGH measures 22°?

6. What is the measure of ∠KGF if ∠EGK measures 68°?

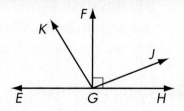

For **7 and 8**, use the diagram at the right.

7. Joe makes a design by turning quadrilateral ABCD 72° about point A. He rotates it 72° about point A again. What is the measure of ∠DAZ?

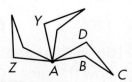

8. The measure of ∠YAD is 72°. The measure of ∠YAB is 95°. What is the measure of ∠DAB?

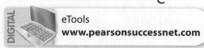

eTools
www.pearsonsuccessnet.com

∠EBC and ∠ABE do not overlap, so the measure of right angle ABC is equal to the sum of the measures of its parts.

The measure of ∠ABC equals the measure of ∠ABE plus the measure of ∠EBC.

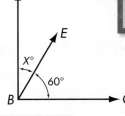

Tip *All right angles measure 90°.*

Write an equation to find the missing angle measure:

$$x + 60 = 90$$

Solve the equation.

$$x = 90 - 60 = 30$$

$$x = 30$$

The measure of ∠ABE is 30°.

So, Elinor uses subtraction instead of a protractor to find the measure of ∠ABE.

Problem Solving

MATHEMATICAL
PRACTICES

Ⓒ **9. Mental Math** Alex draws an angle that measures 110°. He then draws a ray that divides the angle into 2 equal parts. What is the measure of each smaller angle?

10. Talia receives a total of 85¢ for cans she recycles. If she gets a nickel for each can, how many cans does she recycle?

Ⓒ **11. Use Tools** Li uses pattern blocks to make a design. He puts 5 parallelogram blocks together, as shown in the diagram. The measure of ∠LJK is 30°. Use this information and the diagram to answer the following questions.

  a What is the measure of ∠MJK?

  b What is the measure of ∠NJK?

  c What is the measure of ∠OJK?

  d What is the measure of ∠PJK?

Tip *Remember the parallelograms have the same angle measures.*

12. Write 5 hundredths as a decimal and as a fraction.

13. Twenty equal angles share a vertex. The sum of the measures of the angles is 360°. What is the measure of one angle?

Ⓒ **14. Reason** ∠EFG is divided into 2 parts by a ray. One of the smaller angles formed is an obtuse angle and the other is an acute angle. Which of these cannot be the measure of ∠EFG?

  A 89°   **B** 98°   **C** 109°   **D** 118°

Common Core

4.NF.1 Explain why a fraction *a/b* is equivalent to a fraction (*n* × *a*)/(*n* × *b*) by using visual fraction models, with attention to how the number and size of the parts differ even though the two fractions themselves are the same size. Use this principle to recognize and generate equivalent fractions.
Also **4.NF.2**

Number Lines and Equivalent Fractions

How can you find equivalent fractions on a number line?

Sal rode his bike $\frac{3}{4}$ of a mile to school. What is another name for $\frac{3}{4}$?

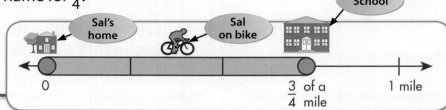

Guided Practice

MATHEMATICAL PRACTICES

Do you know HOW?

In **1** through **3**, find an equivalent fraction on the number line.

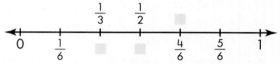

1. Name an equivalent fraction for $\frac{1}{3}$.

2. Name an equivalent fraction for $\frac{1}{2}$.

3. Name an equivalent fraction for $\frac{4}{6}$.

Do you UNDERSTAND?

4. A number line is divided into 12 equal parts to show twelfths. A point is labeled $\frac{1}{2}$. Name two equivalent fractions for the labeled point.

© 5. **Writing to Explain** Use the number line above to name an equivalent fraction for $\frac{1}{4}$. Why are they equivalent?

Independent Practice

MATHEMATICAL PRACTICES

For **6** through **9**, use the number line to name equivalent fractions.

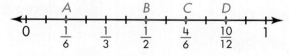

6. Which of the following names an equivalent fraction for point *A*?
$\frac{3}{4}$ $\frac{2}{3}$ $\frac{2}{12}$ $\frac{1}{4}$

© 7. **Be Precise** Which of the following does NOT name an equivalent fraction for point *B*?
$\frac{2}{4}$ $\frac{3}{6}$ $\frac{4}{10}$ $\frac{6}{12}$

8. Which of the following names an equivalent fraction for point *C*?
$\frac{2}{6}$ $\frac{2}{3}$ $\frac{1}{2}$ $\frac{3}{4}$

9. Which of the following names an equivalent fraction for point *D*?
$\frac{4}{6}$ $\frac{1}{2}$ $\frac{1}{10}$ $\frac{5}{6}$

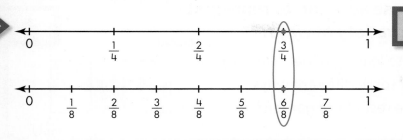

Show $\frac{3}{4}$ on a number line. Divide each fourth in half to show eighths. Find the fraction that names the same point as $\frac{3}{4}$.

Since $\frac{3}{4}$ and $\frac{6}{8}$ name the same point on a number line, they are equivalent fractions.

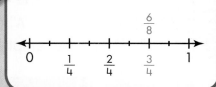

10. Draw a number line to show that $\frac{2}{5}$ and $\frac{4}{10}$ are equivalent fractions.

11. Draw a number line to show that $\frac{1}{3}$ and $\frac{4}{12}$ are equivalent fractions.

Problem Solving

Ⓒ **12. Writing to Explain** How can a number line be used to show that $\frac{2}{10} = \frac{1}{5}$?

13. Name two fractions that represent point Y.

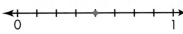

14. In its entire lifetime, the average worker bee produces only $\frac{1}{2}$ of a teaspoon of honey. What is another fraction that names the same amount?

15. At the school fair, 147 tickets were sold. The tickets cost $3 each. The goal was to make $300 in ticket sales. By how much was the goal exceeded?

Ⓒ **16. Be Precise** Which of the following fractions does NOT name the same point on the number line?

17. There are 267 students and 21 adults going on a school trip. An equal number of people will ride on each bus. If there are 9 buses, how many people will ride on each bus?

A $\frac{1}{2}$　**B** $\frac{3}{6}$　**C** $\frac{4}{8}$　**D** $\frac{3}{12}$

Ⓒ **18. Use Structure** Which of the following can help you find a fraction equivalent to $\frac{4}{6}$?

A Subtract the numerator from the denominator.

C Multiply the numerator and the denominator by the same number.

B Add the numerator and the denominator.

D Multiply the numerator by 4 and the denominator by 6.

© Common Core

4.NF.3.b Decompose a fraction into a sum of fractions with the same denominator in more than one way, recording each decomposition by an equation. Justify decompositions, e.g., by using a visual fraction model. Also **4.NF.3.d**

Decomposing and Composing Fractions

How can you use addition to represent a fraction in a variety of ways?

Charlene wants to leave $\frac{1}{6}$ of her garden empty. What are some different ways she can plant the rest of her garden?

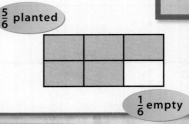

$\frac{5}{6}$ planted

$\frac{1}{6}$ empty

Another Example **How can you use addition to show a mixed number in a variety of ways?**

Jeanie had $3\frac{1}{8}$ sections of a garden to divide equally. How can you use addition to show $3\frac{1}{8}$ as a composition of fractions?

Each whole can be shown as eight equal parts.

$$3\frac{1}{8} = \frac{8}{8} + \frac{8}{8} + \frac{8}{8} + \frac{1}{8}$$

Guided Practice

© MATHEMATICAL PRACTICES

Do you know HOW?

Write each of the following fractions or mixed numbers as a sum of two or three fractions in two different ways.

1. $\frac{3}{5} = \boxed{} + \boxed{}$ $\frac{3}{5} = \boxed{} + \boxed{} + \boxed{}$

2. $1\frac{3}{4} = \boxed{} + \boxed{}$ $1\frac{3}{4} = \boxed{} + \boxed{} + \boxed{}$

Do you UNDERSTAND?

3. Draw a picture to show why both of these equations are true.

$\frac{5}{6} = \frac{3}{6} + \frac{2}{6}$ $\frac{5}{6} = \frac{1}{6} + \frac{2}{6} + \frac{2}{6}$

© **4. Critique Reasoning** Remegio said that the sum for $\frac{1}{10} + \frac{7}{10} + \frac{4}{10}$ is the same as $\frac{5}{10} + \frac{5}{10} + \frac{2}{10}$. Is he correct? Explain.

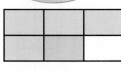

One Way

She could plant 4 sections of blue flowers and 1 section of red peppers.

$\frac{5}{6}$ planted

$\frac{1}{6}$ empty

$$\frac{5}{6} = \frac{4}{6} + \frac{1}{6}$$

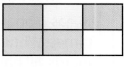

Another Way

She could plant 1 section of green beans, 1 section of yellow squash, 1 section of red peppers, and 2 sections of blue flowers.

$\frac{5}{6}$ planted

$\frac{1}{6}$ empty

$$\frac{5}{6} = \frac{1}{6} + \frac{1}{6} + \frac{1}{6} + \frac{2}{6}$$

Independent Practice

For **5** through **12** find the sum. Then write another addition problem that has the same sum and uses two or more fractions.

5. $\frac{1}{4} + \frac{3}{4} + \frac{3}{4}$

6. $\frac{3}{5} + \frac{3}{5} + \frac{1}{5}$

7. $\frac{3}{10} + \frac{3}{10} + \frac{2}{10}$

8. $\frac{2}{3} + \frac{2}{3} + \frac{1}{3}$

9. $1\frac{1}{2} + \frac{1}{2} + 2\frac{1}{2}$

10. $\frac{3}{6} + \frac{1}{6} + \frac{1}{6}$

11. $\frac{5}{8} + \frac{7}{8} + \frac{3}{8}$

12. $\frac{4}{12} + \frac{6}{12} + \frac{1}{12}$

Problem Solving

MATHEMATICAL
PRACTICES

13. DeAnna walked $\frac{1}{8}$ mile to the park, then $\frac{4}{8}$ mile to the store, and finally $\frac{2}{8}$ mile home. How far did DeAnna walk in all?

A $\frac{5}{8}$ mile

C $\frac{7}{8}$ mile

B $\frac{6}{8}$ mile

D $1\frac{1}{8}$ miles

14. Justin read $\frac{2}{6}$ of his book on Monday, $\frac{1}{6}$ of his book on Tuesday, and $\frac{2}{6}$ of his book on Saturday. How much of his book did Justin read in all?

A $\frac{3}{6}$

C $1\frac{5}{6}$

B $\frac{5}{6}$

D $2\frac{2}{6}$

15. Persevere Serena is wrapping presents, she has $\frac{3}{4}$ yard of red ribbons for wrapping. If she used $\frac{1}{4}$ yard of red ribbon to wrap a present and $\frac{1}{4}$ yard of red ribbon to decorate a card, what fraction amount of ribbon is left?

A $\frac{1}{4}$ yard

C $\frac{3}{4}$ yard

B $\frac{2}{4}$ yard

D $1\frac{1}{4}$ yards

16. Model At the first stop, a bus picks up $\frac{2}{5}$ of the number of passengers it can carry. At the second stop, it picks up $\frac{3}{5}$ of the number of passengers it can carry. If the bus drops off $\frac{1}{5}$ of its passengers on the third stop, what fraction of the total number of passengers will be left? Use fraction strips to model.

Lesson
11-5A
© Common Core

4.NF.3.c Add and subtract mixed numbers with like denominators, e.g., by replacing each mixed number with an equivalent fraction, and/or by using properties of operations and the relationship between addition and subtraction. Also 4.NF.3.b

Modeling Addition and Subtraction of Mixed Numbers

Hands-On fraction strips

$\frac{1}{8}$

How can you model addition of mixed numbers?

Jill has 2 boards she will use to make picture frames. What is the total length of the boards Jill has to make picture frames?

Choose an Operation Add to find the total length.

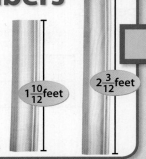

$1\frac{10}{12}$feet $2\frac{3}{12}$feet

Another Example How can you model subtraction of mixed numbers?

Find $2\frac{3}{8} - 1\frac{7}{8}$.

Step 1

Model the number you are subtracting from, $2\frac{3}{8}$.

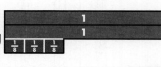

If the fraction you will be subtracting is greater than the fraction of the number you model, rename 1 whole.

Since $\frac{7}{8} > \frac{3}{8}$, rename 1 whole as $\frac{8}{8}$.

Step 2

Use your renamed model to cross out the number that you are subtracting, $1\frac{7}{8}$.

There are $\frac{4}{8}$ left.

So, $2\frac{3}{8} - 1\frac{7}{8} = \frac{4}{8}$.

Simplify: $\frac{4}{8} = \frac{1}{2}$

Explain It

1. In the example above, why is $2\frac{3}{8}$ renamed as $1\frac{11}{8}$?

Guided Practice

Do you know HOW?

Use fraction strips to find each sum or difference. Simplify, if possible.

1. $2\frac{3}{5} + 1\frac{4}{5}$
2. $4\frac{1}{4} - 3\frac{3}{4}$
3. $5\frac{1}{6} - 3\frac{3}{6}$
4. $3\frac{2}{3} + 2\frac{2}{3}$

Do you UNDERSTAND?

5. How is renaming to add mixed numbers different from regrouping to add whole numbers?

6. When adding two mixed numbers is it always necessary to rename the fractional sum? Explain.

Model the addends and add the fractional parts.

$2\frac{3}{12}$

$+ 1\frac{10}{12}$

$\frac{13}{12}$

Rename $\frac{13}{12}$ as $1\frac{1}{12}$.

Now add the whole numbers, including the renamed fraction.

$2 + 1 + 1 = 4$

So, $2\frac{3}{12} + 1\frac{10}{12} = 4\frac{1}{12}$.

The total length of the boards is $4\frac{1}{12}$ feet.

Independent Practice

MATHEMATICAL PRACTICES

In **7** and **8**, use each model to find the sum or difference. Simplify if possible.

7. Charles used $1\frac{1}{3}$ cups of blueberries and $2\frac{1}{3}$ cups of cranberries to make breakfast bread. How many cups of blueberries and cranberries did he use in all?

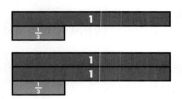

8. Eva ran to her friend's apartment in $2\frac{4}{6}$ minutes. It took Eva $4\frac{3}{6}$ minutes to go back home. How much more time did Eva take to get home?

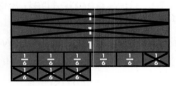

Use Tools In **9** through **16**, use fraction strips to find each sum or difference. Simplify if possible.

9. $5\frac{3}{6} - 2\frac{4}{6}$ **10.** $2\frac{2}{5} + 3\frac{4}{5}$ **11.** $4\frac{9}{10} + 3\frac{7}{10}$ **12.** $1\frac{1}{3} + 3\frac{2}{3}$

13. $1\frac{3}{4} + 2\frac{2}{4}$ **14.** $12\frac{3}{8} - 9\frac{5}{8}$ **15.** $2\frac{5}{12} + 4\frac{7}{12}$ **16.** $13\frac{7}{9} - 10\frac{8}{9}$

eTools
www.pearsonsuccessnet.com

DIGITAL

For **17** and **18**, use fraction strips to solve. Simplify, if possible.

17. Jim said, "On summer vacation, I spent $1\frac{3}{4}$ months with my grandma and $\frac{3}{4}$ month with my aunt."

    a How many months is that in all?

    b How many months longer did Jim spend with his grandmother than with his aunt?

18. Ethan used $1\frac{2}{3}$ gallons of yellow paint for the ceiling and $3\frac{2}{3}$ gallons of blue paint for the walls of his kitchen.

    a How much paint did Ethan use in all?

    b How much more blue paint did Ethan use than yellow paint?

For **19** through **21**, use the table at the right.

19. Sarah is making costumes for the school play. Write the amount of material for a peasant blouse as a mixed number.

20. Which costume requires the most fabric?

21. Which costume requires the least fabric?

Costume Shopping List	
Costume	**Yards**
Peasant skirt	$\frac{12}{3}$
Peasant vest	$\frac{9}{8}$
Peasant blouse	$\frac{9}{4}$

Data

ⓒ **22.** **Generalize** What is the value of the underlined digit in 62<u>7</u>?

    A 7 ten thousands   **B** 7 thousands   **C** 7 tens   **D** 7 ones

For **23** and **24**, use the table at the right.

23. 🥄 Science How many inches longer is a Hercules beetle than a ladybug?

24. What is the difference between the largest and the smallest stag beetles? What is the sum of their lengths?

Beetles by Length	
Beetle	**Length in inches**
Hercules beetle	$6\frac{3}{4}$
Ladybug	$\frac{1}{4}$
Stag beetle	$1\frac{1}{8}$ to $2\frac{4}{8}$

Data

25. Nicole, Tasha, Maria, and Joan ran a relay race. Nicole ran the first leg of the race in $1\frac{5}{6}$ minutes. Tasha ran the second leg in $2\frac{1}{6}$ minutes. Maria ran the third leg in $1\frac{5}{6}$ minutes. Joan ran the last leg in $2\frac{1}{6}$ minutes to finish the race.

ⓒ   **a** **Reason** How can you find how much faster Maria ran than Joan?

    b The team wanted to run the race in less than six minutes. Did they meet their goal? Explain.

Different musical instruments make different sounds. The shape of an instrument can affect how it sounds. Use the table at the right to answer **1–4**.

1. Which instrument is made up of a long, narrow rectangular prism and a short cylinder?

2. Which of the percussion instruments has a cylinder shape?

3. Which instrument has the shape of a 3-sided figure?

4. What solid does the recorder look like?

5. The instrument that makes the sound with the greatest number of decibels is the loudest. Which instrument in the table below can make the loudest sound?

Instrument	Maximum Loudness (in decibels)
Trumpet	95
Cymbal	110
Bass drum	115
Piano	100

Data

Musical Instruments

Name of Instrument		Group of Instruments
Banjo		String
Drum		Percussion
Recorder		Woodwind
Triangle		Percussion

. . . .

© 6. **Persevere** Solve. Use the strategy Work Backward.

Elian plays three instruments. The drum weighs 5 pounds more than the guitar. The trumpet weighs 5 pounds less than the guitar. The trumpet weighs 3 pounds. How many pounds does the drum weigh?

Lesson
11-5B

©
Common Core

4.NF.3.c Add and subtract mixed numbers with like denominators, e.g., by replacing each mixed number with an equivalent fraction, and/or by using properties of operations and the relationship between addition and subtraction.

Adding Mixed Numbers

How can you add mixed numbers?

Brenda mixes sand with $2\frac{7}{8}$ cups of potting mixture to prepare soil for her plants. After mixing them together, how many cups of soil does Brenda have?

Choose an Operation Add to find the total amount of soil.

$1\frac{3}{8}$ cups

Another Example **How can you check for reasonableness?**

You just found that the sum of $2\frac{7}{8}$ and $1\frac{3}{8}$ is $4\frac{1}{4}$. You can use estimation to check that a sum is reasonable.

Estimate $2\frac{7}{8} + 1\frac{3}{8}$.

A number line can help you replace mixed numbers with the nearest one-half or whole unit.

$2\frac{7}{8}$ is close to 3.

$1\frac{3}{8}$ is close to $1\frac{1}{2}$.

Add: $3 + 1\frac{1}{2} = 4\frac{1}{2}$

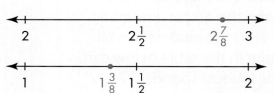

Since both of the addends were replaced with larger numbers for the estimate, the actual answer will be less.

The actual sum, $4\frac{1}{4}$, is reasonable because it is close to the estimate, $4\frac{1}{2}$.

Guided Practice

MATHEMATICAL
PRACTICES

Do you know HOW?

Find each sum. Simplify, if possible. Estimate to check for reasonableness.

1. $1\frac{7}{8}$
   $+ 1\frac{2}{8}$

2. $2\frac{4}{10}$
   $+ 5\frac{5}{10}$

3. $4\frac{2}{3} + 1\frac{2}{3}$

4. $6\frac{5}{12} + 4\frac{11}{12}$

Do you UNDERSTAND?

© 5. **Reason** How is adding mixed numbers like adding fractions and whole numbers?

© 6. **Writing to Explain** Alan used 9 as an estimate for $3\frac{7}{10} + 5\frac{4}{10}$. He added and got $9\frac{1}{10}$ for the actual sum. Is his answer reasonable?

<table>
<tr><td>

Step 1

Find $2\frac{7}{8} + 1\frac{3}{8}$. Add the fractions.

$2\frac{7}{8}$ [▓ ⅛ ⅛ ⅛ ⅛ ⅛ ⅛ ⅛]

$+ 1\frac{3}{8}$ [⅛ ⅛ ⅛]

$\dfrac{10}{8}$ [⅛ ⅛ ⅛ ⅛ ⅛ ⅛ ⅛ ⅛ ⅛ ⅛]

</td><td>

Step 2

Add the whole numbers. Simplify the sum if possible.

$2\frac{7}{8}$

$+ 1\frac{3}{8}$

$3\frac{10}{8}$

$$3\frac{10}{8} = 4\frac{2}{8} = 4\frac{1}{4}$$

Brenda prepared $4\frac{1}{4}$ cups of soil.

</td></tr>
</table>

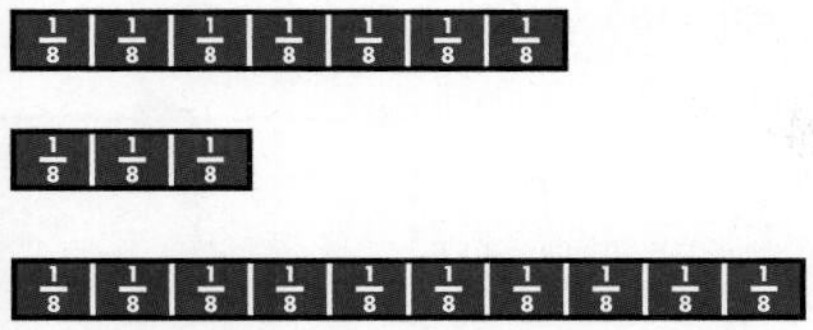

Independent Practice

Leveled Practice For **7** through **18**, find each sum and simplify, if possible. Check for reasonableness.

7. $2\frac{5}{6}$
$+ 5\frac{4}{6}$
_____

8. $11\frac{7}{10}$
$+ 10\frac{9}{10}$
_____

9. $9\frac{7}{8}$
$+ 7\frac{5}{8}$
_____

10. $5\frac{7}{8}$
$+ 8\frac{1}{8}$
_____

11. $4\frac{1}{10} + 6\frac{5}{10}$

12. $9\frac{7}{12} + 4\frac{9}{12}$

13. $5 + 3\frac{1}{8}$

14. $8\frac{3}{4} + 7\frac{3}{4}$

15. $2\frac{4}{5} + 7\frac{3}{5}$

16. $3\frac{2}{6} + 8\frac{5}{6}$

17. $1\frac{7}{12} + 2\frac{10}{12}$

18. $3\frac{6}{8} + 9\frac{3}{8}$

Problem Solving

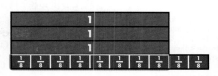
MATHEMATICAL PRACTICES

© **19. Persevere** Joe biked $1\frac{9}{12}$ miles from home to the lake, then went $1\frac{3}{12}$ miles around the lake, and then back home. How many miles did he bike?

A $2\frac{1}{12}$ miles

B $3\frac{1}{12}$ miles

C $4\frac{3}{4}$ miles

D $4\frac{5}{12}$ miles

20. a Use the map below to find the distance from the start of the trail to the end.

b Linda walked from the start of the trail to the bird lookout and back. Did she walk more or less than if she had walked from the start of the trail to the end?

21. The length of a male Parson's chameleon can be up to $23\frac{2}{4}$ inches. It can extend its tongue up to $35\frac{1}{4}$ inches to catch its food. What is the total length of a male Parson's chameleon when its tongue is fully extended?

Lesson

11-5C

© Common Core

4.NF.3.c Add and subtract mixed numbers with like denominators, e.g., by replacing each mixed number with an equivalent fraction, and/or by using properties of operations and the relationship between addition and subtraction.

Subtracting Mixed Numbers

How can you subtract mixed numbers?

A golf ball measures about $1\frac{4}{6}$ inches across the center. What is the difference between the distance across the center of a tennis ball and the golf ball?

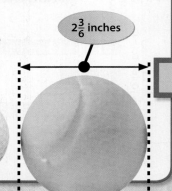

$2\frac{3}{6}$ inches

Choose an Operation Subtract to find the difference.

Another Example **How can you check for reasonableness?**

You just found that the difference of $2\frac{3}{6}$ and $1\frac{4}{6}$ is $\frac{5}{6}$. You can use estimation to check that a difference is reasonable.

Estimate $2\frac{3}{6} - 1\frac{4}{6}$.

$2\frac{3}{6}$ is the same as $2\frac{1}{2}$.

$1\frac{4}{6}$ is close to $1\frac{1}{2}$.

Subtract: $2\frac{1}{2} - 1\frac{1}{2} = 1$.

The actual difference, $\frac{5}{6}$, is reasonable because it is close to the estimate, 1.

Guided Practice

© MATHEMATICAL PRACTICES

Do you know HOW?

Find each difference and simplify, if possible. Check for reasonableness.

1. $7\frac{3}{8} = 6\frac{\ \ }{8}$
    $-2\frac{4}{8} = 2\frac{\ \ }{8}$

2. $5 \quad = \frac{\ \ \ }{4}$
    $-2\frac{3}{4} = \quad 2\frac{3}{4}$

3. $6\frac{3}{10} - 1\frac{8}{10}$

4. $9\frac{4}{12} - 4\frac{9}{12}$

Do you UNDERSTAND?

5. In Exercise 2, why do you need to rename the 5?

© 6. **Reasonableness** Could two golf balls fall into a hole that is $3\frac{3}{6}$ inches across at the same time? Explain your reasoning.

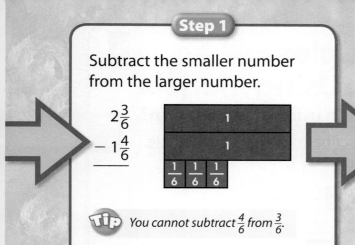

Step 1

Subtract the smaller number from the larger number.

$$2\frac{3}{6}$$
$$-1\frac{4}{6}$$
$$\overline{}$$

Tip You cannot subtract $\frac{4}{6}$ from $\frac{3}{6}$.

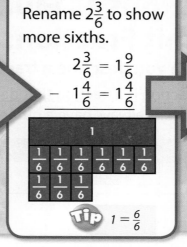

Step 2

Rename $2\frac{3}{6}$ to show more sixths.

$$2\frac{3}{6} = 1\frac{9}{6}$$
$$-1\frac{4}{6} = 1\frac{4}{6}$$
$$\overline{}$$

Tip $1 = \frac{6}{6}$

Step 3

Subtract the fractions. Then subtract the whole numbers.

$$2\frac{3}{6} = 1\frac{9}{6}$$
$$-1\frac{4}{6} = 1\frac{4}{6}$$
$$\overline{\frac{5}{6}}$$

The tennis ball is $\frac{5}{6}$ inch wider.

Independent Practice

Leveled Practice For **7** through **18**, find each difference and simplify, if possible. Check for reasonableness.

7. $\quad 8\frac{2}{8} = 7\frac{\boxed{}}{8}$
$\quad\; - 2\frac{7}{8} = 2\frac{\boxed{}}{8}$
$\quad\; \overline{}$

8. $\quad 4\frac{5}{10} = 3\frac{\boxed{}}{10}$
$\quad\; -1\frac{9}{10} = 1\frac{\boxed{}}{10}$
$\quad\; \overline{}$

9. $\quad 4\frac{1}{8}$
$\quad\; - 1\frac{4}{8}$
$\quad\; \overline{}$

10. $\quad 6$
$\quad\; - 2\frac{4}{5}$
$\quad\; \overline{}$

11. $6\frac{1}{3} - 5\frac{2}{3}$

12. $9\frac{2}{4} - 6\frac{3}{4}$

13. $8\frac{3}{8} - 3\frac{5}{8}$

14. $7 - 3\frac{1}{2}$

15. $15\frac{1}{6} - 4\frac{5}{6}$

16. $13\frac{1}{12} - 8\frac{3}{12}$

17. $6\frac{2}{5} - 2\frac{3}{5}$

18. $10\frac{5}{10} - 4\frac{7}{10}$

Problem Solving

MATHEMATICAL
PRACTICES

19. The average weight of a basketball is $21\frac{1}{8}$ ounces. The average weight of a baseball is $5\frac{2}{8}$ ounces. How many more ounces does the basketball weigh?

   A $15\frac{1}{8}$ **B** $15\frac{7}{8}$ **C** $16\frac{1}{8}$ **D** $16\frac{7}{8}$

Ⓒ **20. Reason** As of 2008, the world's shortest horse is Thumbelina. She is $17\frac{1}{4}$ inches tall. The second shortest horse, Black Beauty, is $18\frac{2}{4}$ inches tall. How much shorter is Thumbelina than Black Beauty?

21. The smallest mammals on Earth are the bumblebee bat and the Etruscan pygmy shrew. The length of a bumblebee bat is $1\frac{1}{5}$ inches. The length of an Etruscan pygmy shrew is $1\frac{2}{5}$ inches. How much smaller is the bat than the shrew?

Ⓒ **22. Writing to Explain** How are the parallelogram and the rectangle alike? How are they different?

Common Core

4.NF.4.a Understand a fraction $\frac{a}{b}$ as a multiple of $\frac{1}{b}$.

Hands-On
fraction strips

$\frac{1}{8}$

Fractions as Multiples of Unit Fractions: Using Models

How can you describe a fraction using a unit fraction?

A unit fraction is a fraction that describes one part of the whole. Unit fractions always have a numerator of 1.

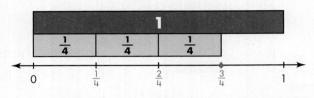

Guided Practice

MATHEMATICAL PRACTICES

Do you know HOW?

For **1** through **4**, write the fraction as a multiple of a unit fraction. Use fraction strips to help.

1. $\frac{2}{3} = \boxed{} \times \frac{1}{3}$ **2.** $\frac{5}{6} = 5 \times \frac{1}{\boxed{}}$

3. $\frac{3}{2} = \boxed{}$ **4.** $\frac{6}{5} = \boxed{}$

Do you UNDERSTAND?

5. Use Structure Draw a picture to explain why $\frac{8}{5} = 8 \times \frac{1}{5}$.

6. Write the multiplication equation to show each part of the following story. Mark's family ate $\frac{6}{4}$ chicken pot pies for dinner. There are 6 people in Mark's family. Each family member ate $\frac{1}{4}$ of a pie.

Independent Practice

Leveled Practice For **7** through **22**, write the fraction as a multiple of a unit fraction. Use fraction strips to help.

7. $\frac{3}{4} = \boxed{} \times \frac{1}{4}$ **8.** $\frac{3}{6} = 3 \times \frac{1}{\boxed{}}$ **9.** $\frac{2}{5} = \boxed{} \times \frac{1}{5}$ **10.** $\frac{8}{12} = 8 \times \frac{1}{\boxed{}}$

11. $\frac{7}{10} = \boxed{}$ **12.** $\frac{8}{8} = \boxed{}$ **13.** $\frac{5}{12} = \boxed{}$ **14.** $\frac{6}{6} = \boxed{}$

15. $\frac{6}{4} = \boxed{}$ **16.** $\frac{9}{6} = \boxed{}$ **17.** $\frac{8}{5} = \boxed{}$ **18.** $\frac{9}{8} = \boxed{}$

19. $\frac{7}{8} = \boxed{}$ **20.** $\frac{9}{4} = \boxed{}$ **21.** $\frac{8}{6} = \boxed{}$ **22.** $\frac{35}{100} = \boxed{}$

DIGITAL
eTools
www.pearsonsuccessnet.com

When a whole is divided into four equal parts, each part is described as $\frac{1}{4}$.

Three of those parts are described as $\frac{3}{4}$.

Multiplication and a unit fraction also can be used to describe $\frac{3}{4}$.

$\frac{3}{4} = 3 \times \frac{1}{4}$, or three $\frac{1}{4}$ parts.

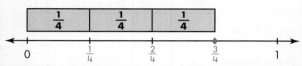

Three $\frac{1}{4}$ parts make $\frac{3}{4}$.

$$\frac{3}{4} = 3 \times \frac{1}{4}$$

So, $\frac{3}{4}$ is a multiple of $\frac{1}{4}$.

A multiple is the result of multiplying a number by a whole number.

Problem Solving

MATHEMATICAL
PRACTICES

23. Model Write an equation that describes the picture below. Show your answer as a multiplication equation with a unit fraction as a factor.

24. Write a Problem Look at the picture. Write and solve a problem for it. Show your answer as a multiplication equation with $\frac{1}{2}$ as a factor.

25. Leslie is baking bread. The recipe calls for $1\frac{3}{4}$ cups of all-purpose flour and $1\frac{1}{4}$ cups of whole wheat flour. How many cups of flour does Leslie need in all?

   A $\frac{1}{2}$

   B 2

   C 3

   D $3\frac{1}{4}$

26. Mari is packing oranges into bags. She packs the same number of oranges in each bag. The table below shows the number of oranges she packs for different numbers of bags. How many oranges does Mari need to pack 9 bags?

Number of Bags	3	5	7	9	11
Number of Oranges	9	15	21		33

27. Use Structure Kevin is baking cookies. Each batch of cookies uses $\frac{1}{8}$ pound of butter. Kevin has $1\frac{3}{8}$ pounds of butter. How many batches of cookies can he make? Show your answer as a multiplication equation with $\frac{1}{8}$ as a factor.

28. Use Structure Kobe drinks $\frac{1}{3}$ cup of grapefruit juice each morning. He has $2\frac{1}{3}$ cups of juice left. For how many mornings will it last? Show your answer as a multiplication equation with $\frac{1}{3}$ as a factor. (Hint: Write $2\frac{1}{3}$ as an improper fraction.)

4.NF.4.b Understand a multiple of $\frac{a}{b}$ as a multiple of $\frac{1}{b}$, and use this understanding to multiply a fraction by a whole number. Also **4.NF.4**

Multiplying a Fraction by a Whole Number: Using Models

How can you find the product of a fraction multiplied by a whole number?

Doris lives $\frac{1}{4}$ of a mile from school. If she walks to and from school each day, how far does she walk during a school week?

Distance Walked (in miles)					
	Mon	Tues	Wed	Thurs	Fri
To School	$\frac{1}{4}$	$\frac{1}{4}$	$\frac{1}{4}$	$\frac{1}{4}$	$\frac{1}{4}$
From School	$\frac{1}{4}$	$\frac{1}{4}$	$\frac{1}{4}$	$\frac{1}{4}$	$\frac{1}{4}$

Another Example

Show a picture of Doris's walk in another way. Show 5 days of $\frac{2}{4}$ mile walks.

$\frac{1}{4}$	$\frac{1}{4}$	$\frac{1}{4}$	$\frac{1}{4}$	$\frac{1}{4}$	$\frac{1}{4}$	$\frac{1}{4}$	$\frac{1}{4}$	$\frac{1}{4}$	$\frac{1}{4}$
$\frac{2}{4}$		$\frac{2}{4}$		$\frac{2}{4}$		$\frac{2}{4}$		$\frac{2}{4}$	

You can show the total she walks with addition.

$$\frac{2}{4} + \frac{2}{4} + \frac{2}{4} + \frac{2}{4} + \frac{2}{4} = \frac{10}{4} = 2\frac{1}{2}$$

Doris walks $2\frac{1}{2}$ miles each week.

You can also show the total with multiplication.

$$5 \times \frac{2}{4} = 5 \times \left(2 \times \frac{1}{4}\right)$$
$$= (5 \times 2) \times \frac{1}{4}$$
$$= 10 \times \frac{1}{4}$$
$$= \frac{10}{4} \text{ or } 2\frac{2}{4} = 2\frac{1}{2} \text{ miles}$$

Guided Practice

MATHEMATICAL PRACTICES

Do you know HOW?

In **1** and **2**, write a multiplication equation with a whole number and a fraction for each picture.

1.

2.

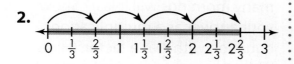

Do you UNDERSTAND?

© **3. Reason** In the example at the top of the page, explain why the total distance Doris walks to school each week can also be found using multiplication.

4. Draw a picture to explain why $3 \times \frac{2}{5} = \frac{(3 \times 2)}{5} = \frac{6}{5}$.

© **5. Reason** What property of multiplication is used to write $5 \times (2 \times \frac{1}{4}) = (5 \times 2) \times \frac{1}{4}$? How does this help you multiply?

Draw a picture to show the distance Doris walks.

$\frac{1}{4}$	$\frac{1}{4}$	$\frac{1}{4}$	$\frac{1}{4}$	$\frac{1}{4}$	$\frac{1}{4}$	$\frac{1}{4}$	$\frac{1}{4}$	$\frac{1}{4}$	$\frac{1}{4}$

0   1   2

$$\frac{1}{4} + \frac{1}{4} + \frac{1}{4} + \frac{1}{4} + \frac{1}{4} + \frac{1}{4} + \frac{1}{4} + \frac{1}{4} + \frac{1}{4} + \frac{1}{4} = \frac{10}{4}$$

Simplify $\frac{10}{4}$.

$$\frac{10}{4} = 2\frac{2}{4} = 2\frac{1}{2}$$

Ten $\frac{1}{4}$ miles added together makes $\frac{10}{4}$ miles, or $2\frac{1}{2}$ miles.

Multiplication can also be used to join equal parts.

$$10 \times \frac{1}{4} = \frac{10}{4} = 2\frac{2}{4} = 2\frac{1}{2}$$

Doris walks $2\frac{1}{2}$ miles to and from school each week.

Independent Practice

In **6** and **7**, write a multiplication equation with a whole number and a fraction for each picture.

6.

$\frac{1}{8}$ mi	$\frac{1}{8}$ mi	$\frac{1}{8}$ mi	$\frac{1}{8}$ mi	$\frac{1}{8}$ mi

7.

$\frac{2}{10}$ $\frac{2}{10}$ $\frac{2}{10}$

Problem Solving

 MATHEMATICAL PRACTICES

© **8. Reason** Kiona fills a measuring cup with $\frac{3}{4}$ cup of juice 3 times. Write and solve a multiplication equation with a whole number and a fraction to show the total amount of juice she uses.

© **9. Model** Each lap around a track is $\frac{3}{10}$ kilometer. Eliot walked around the track 4 times. How far did Eliot walk in all?

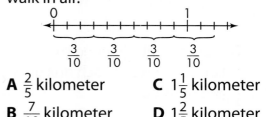

A $\frac{2}{5}$ kilometer   **C** $1\frac{1}{5}$ kilometer

B $\frac{7}{10}$ kilometer   **D** $1\frac{2}{5}$ kilometer

© **10. Persevere** Wendy sliced a loaf of bread into 12 equal slices. She used 4 of the slices to make sandwiches. What fraction of the loaf of bread was left?

11. A pan of lasagna is cut into 6 equal pieces. The chef serves 5 pieces of the lasagna. Write and solve a multiplication equation to show how much of the lasagna is served.

© **12. Communicate** Zach made trail mix using $\frac{1}{8}$ pound of each of the following: walnuts, raisins, almonds, peanuts, sunflower seeds, and dates. What is the total weight of the trail mix? Explain by drawing a picture and writing an equation.

Lesson 11-5F

Common Core

4.NF.4.c Solve word problems involving multiplication of a fraction by a whole number, e.g., by using visual fraction models and equations to represent the problem. Also 4.NF.4, 4.NF.4.b

Multiplying a Fraction by a Whole Number: Using Symbols

When can you use the product of a fraction and a whole number to solve a problem?

At his job at the ice cream counter, Stanley makes large ice cream sundaes that contain $\frac{3}{4}$ pint of ice cream. Today, Stanley made 5 of these sundaes. How much ice cream did he use?

$\frac{3}{4}$ pt of ice cream in each sundae

 **Guided Practice**

 **MATHEMATICAL PRACTICES**

Do you know HOW?

For **1–4**, multiply.

1. $8 \times \frac{1}{2} = \blacksquare$ **2.** $13 \times \frac{3}{4} = \blacksquare$

3. $7 \times \frac{2}{3} = \blacksquare$ **4.** $9 \times \frac{1}{8} = \blacksquare$

For **5** and **6**, write a multiplication equation for each situation.

5. Medicine taken in 10 days if the dose is $\frac{3}{4}$ ounce per day.

6. The total length needed to decorate 9 boxes if each box uses $\frac{2}{3}$ yard of ribbon.

Do you UNDERSTAND?

Write a number sentence that describes each situation.

7. Model Sarah has $\frac{1}{2}$ of a granola bar. Her friend has 5 times as many granola bars. How many granola bars does Sarah's friend have?

8. Model Sue needs $\frac{5}{6}$ cup of cocoa to make one batch of chocolate pudding. She wants to make 4 batches of pudding to take to a party. Write and solve an equation to show how much cocoa Sue will need for all 4 batches of pudding.

Independent Practice

For **9–17**, multiply. Write the product in simplest form.

9. $4 \times \frac{1}{3} = \blacksquare$ **10.** $6 \times \frac{3}{8} = \blacksquare$ **11.** $8 \times \frac{2}{5} = \blacksquare$

12. $12 \times \frac{5}{6} = \blacksquare$ **13.** $11 \times \frac{2}{3} = \blacksquare$ **14.** $5 \times \frac{7}{8} = \blacksquare$

15. $7 \times \frac{3}{4} = \blacksquare$ **16.** $9 \times \frac{3}{5} = \blacksquare$ **17.** $4 \times \frac{5}{8} = \blacksquare$

I am joining 5 groups of $\frac{3}{4}$ of a pint.

$\frac{3}{4} + \frac{3}{4} + \frac{3}{4} + \frac{3}{4} + \frac{3}{4}$

Joining equal-sized groups can be shown with multiplication.

Find $5 \times \frac{3}{4}$.

$5 \times \frac{3}{4} = \frac{(5 \times 3)}{4}$

$= \frac{15}{4}$

$= 3\frac{3}{4}$

Stanley needs $3\frac{3}{4}$ pints of ice cream to make 5 sundaes.

For **18** and **19**, write a number sentence for each situation and find the answer.

18. The total distance Mary runs in one week if she runs $\frac{7}{8}$ mile each day.

19. The length of 5 pieces of ribbon laid end to end if each piece is $\frac{2}{3}$ yard long.

Problem Solving

MATHEMATICAL
PRACTICES

20. Model Malik swims $\frac{9}{10}$ of a mile each day. How many miles will he swim in 8 days? Write a number sentence and solve.

21. Sean is making picture frames. Each frame uses $\frac{4}{5}$ yard of wood. What is the total length of wood Sean will need to make 12 frames?

22. Persevere Sun is making 7 fruit tarts. Each tart needs $\frac{3}{4}$ cup of strawberries and $\frac{1}{4}$ cup of blueberries. What is the total amount of fruit that Sun needs for her tarts?

23. Writing to Explain Lydia is making 4 loaves of rye bread and 3 loaves of wheat bread. Each loaf takes $\frac{3}{4}$ cup of sugar. What is the total amount of sugar Lydia will need? Explain.

24. Write a story to go along with the multiplication sentence $3 \times \frac{3}{10}$. Then, solve your problem.

25. Reason Olivia is doing her math homework. For each problem, she uses $\frac{3}{4}$ of a sheet of paper. How many sheets of paper will she need to complete 20 problems?

A 4 sheets **C** 15 sheets

B $5\frac{3}{4}$ sheets **D** $20\frac{3}{4}$ sheets

26. It takes Mario $\frac{1}{4}$ hour to mow Mr. Harris's lawn. It takes him 3 times as long to mow Mrs. Carter's lawn. How long does it take Mario to mow Mrs. Carter's lawn?

Equivalent Fractions and Decimals

How can you use equivalent fractions to change a fraction to a decimal?

A pan of cornbread was divided into 12 equal pieces, and 6 out of 12 pieces or $\frac{6}{12}$ of the cornbread remains. Write a fraction equivalent to $\frac{6}{12}$, and then change the fraction to a decimal.

Other Examples

Write $\frac{3}{12}$ as a decimal.

In simplest form $\frac{3}{12}$ is $\frac{1}{4}$.

Find an equivalent fraction with a denominator of 100.

Think 4 times what number equals 100?

$$\overset{\times\, 25}{\overset{\frown}{\frac{1}{4} = \frac{25}{100}}}$$
$$\underset{\times\, 25}{}$$

$\frac{25}{100}$ is twenty-five hundredths, or 0.25.

So, $\frac{3}{12}$ = 0.25.

Write 0.8 as a fraction in simplest form.

0.8 is eight tenths, or $\frac{8}{10}$.

Simplify the fraction $\frac{8}{10}$.

Think 8 and 10 are multiples of what number?

$$\overset{\div\, 2}{\overset{\frown}{\frac{8}{10} = \frac{4}{5}}}$$
$$\underset{\div\, 2}{}$$

0.8 is eight tenths, or $\frac{4}{5}$.

So, 0.8 = $\frac{4}{5}$.

Explain It

© **1. Reason** Why is the fraction $\frac{1}{2}$ not written as 0.12?

2. What steps would you take to rename $\frac{2}{4}$ as an equivalent fraction with a denominator of 100?

In simplest form $\frac{6}{12}$ is $\frac{1}{2}$. Find an equivalent fraction with a denominator of 10.

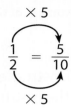

Think 2 times what number equals 10?

$$\frac{1}{2} \overset{\times 5}{\underset{\times 5}{=}} \frac{5}{10}$$

$\frac{1}{2} = \frac{5}{10}$

$\frac{5}{10}$ is five tenths, or 0.5.

So, 0.5 of the cornbread remains.

Write $\frac{3}{4}$ as a decimal.

Multiply to find an equivalent fraction with a denominator of 100.

Think 4 times what number equals 100?

$$\frac{3}{4} \overset{\times 25}{\underset{\times 25}{=}} \frac{75}{100}$$

$\frac{3}{4} = \frac{75}{100}$

$\frac{75}{100}$ is seventy-five hundredths, or 0.75.

Guided Practice

MATHEMATICAL PRACTICES

Do you know HOW?

For **1** through **6**, write each fraction as a decimal.

1. $\frac{3}{5} = \frac{\blacksquare}{10}$

2. $\frac{2}{4} = \frac{50}{\blacksquare}$

3. $\frac{1}{5}$

4. $\frac{3}{12}$

5. $\frac{2}{8}$

6. $\frac{3}{5}$

Do you UNDERSTAND?

7. Write a fraction and an equivalent decimal to show the part of the cornbread that has been eaten.

ⓒ **8. Writing to Explain** When you write a fraction as a decimal, why do you need to rename the fraction as an equivalent fraction with a denominator of 10 or 100?

Independent Practice

In **9** through **18**, write each fraction as a decimal.

9. $\frac{2}{5} = \frac{\blacksquare}{10}$

10. $\frac{4}{5} = \frac{\blacksquare}{10}$

11. $\frac{4}{5} = \frac{8}{\blacksquare}$

12. $\frac{2}{8} = \frac{\blacksquare}{100}$

13. $\frac{7}{100} = \frac{\blacksquare}{100}$

14. $\frac{3}{12}$

15. $\frac{6}{10}$

16. $\frac{4}{10}$

17. $\frac{1}{5}$

18. $\frac{35}{100}$

In **19** through **30**, tell whether each pair shows equivalent numbers.

19. $\frac{4}{8}$, 0.5

20. $\frac{1}{5}$, 0.15

21. $\frac{65}{100}$, 0.65

22. $\frac{2}{4}$, 0.35

23. $\frac{4}{8}$, 0.08

24. $\frac{6}{12}$, 0.6

25. $\frac{4}{8}$, 0.5

26. $\frac{8}{100}$, 0.08

27. $\frac{3}{12}$, 0.25

28. $\frac{3}{10}$, 0.03

29. $\frac{4}{5}$, 0.8

30. $\frac{1}{2}$, 0.05

31. Roger got 24 hits out of 100 times at bat. What is his batting average as a fraction in simplest form? Then write an equivalent decimal.

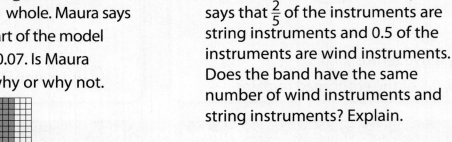

$$\text{Batting Average} = \frac{\text{Number of hits}}{\text{Number of times at bat}}$$

© **32. Critique Reasoning** The model below represents 1 whole. Maura says that the shaded part of the model shows that $\frac{70}{100} = 0.07$. Is Maura correct? Explain why or why not.

33. A band has 20 instruments. Tyler says that $\frac{2}{5}$ of the instruments are string instruments and 0.5 of the instruments are wind instruments. Does the band have the same number of wind instruments and string instruments? Explain.

34. Gina wrote a 4-digit number. She used each of the digits 1, 3, 5, and 7 once. How many different 4-digit numbers can Gina write?

© **35. Writing to Explain** Which is greater, $\frac{3}{4}$ or 0.75? Explain your answer.

© **36. Reason** The cell phone was invented in Sweden in 1979. How many years ago was the cell phone invented?

37. Write a fraction in simplest form and an equivalent decimal to show what part of a dollar 5 cents represents. (Hint: 1 dollar = 100 cents.)

For **38**, use the diagram at the right.

38. Kwan has 37 customers on his paper route. He delivers newspapers every day. How many newspapers does he deliver in one week?

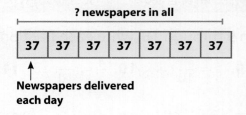

© **39. Reasonableness** Betty's score on a 5-point quiz was 4 out of 5, or $\frac{4}{5}$. What is $\frac{4}{5}$ written as a decimal?

A 0.4

B 0.45

C 0.6

D 0.8

40. Nine of the 12 students in the school play are fourth graders. Which decimal represents the part of the students that are fourth graders?

A 0.25

B 0.6

C 0.75

D 0.9

Solve each equation for z.

1. $z + 22 = 24$ **2.** $z - 19 = 24$ **3.** $z \times 4 = 32$

4. $z \div 9 = 4$ **5.** $15 + z = 24$ **6.** $z - 22 = 22$

7. $6 \times z = 6$ **8.** $z \div 5 = 1$ **9.** $3 \times z = 18$

Round each decimal to the nearest tenth.

10. 9.64   **11.** 1.05   **12.** 3.52   **13.** 16.67   **14.** 87.24

Find the sum. Estimate to check if the answer is reasonable.

15. $9 + 3{,}529 + 27 + 621$ **16.** $17{,}868 + 913 + 2{,}781$

17. $475 + 25 + 5{,}350 + 25{,}275$ **18.** $2 + 129 + 56 + 374$

ⓒ **Reason** Find each value of *w* that is not correct.
Write it correctly, and explain the error.

19. $20 + w = 68$ **20.** $w - 12 = 50$ **21.** $w \div 2 = 9$ **22.** $w \times 6 = 42$
    $w = 88$ $w = 62$ $w = 11$ $w = 8$

Number Sense

ⓒ **Construct Arguments** Write whether each
statement is true or false. Explain your answer.

23. The expression $101 - 25$ equals 76.

24. The product of 4 and 682 is closer to 2,400 than 2,800.

25. The sum of 251 and 173 is less than 400.

26. The quotient of 0 divided by 1 is 1.

27. The product of 5 and 45 is 25 more than 200.

28. The difference of 844 and 172 is greater than 600.

Lesson
14-7A

Common Core

4.MD.3 Apply the area and perimeter formulas for rectangles in real world and mathematical problems.

Solving Perimeter and Area Problems

How can you use perimeter and area to solve problems?

Perimeter is the distance around a figure. Area is the amount of surface a figure covers. What is the area of the new state park shown at the right?

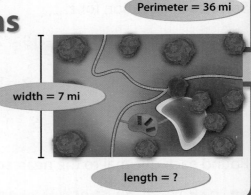

Perimeter = 36 mi

width = 7 mi

length = ?

Guided Practice

Do you know HOW?

Find the missing dimension or dimensions.

1.

Area = 216 sq in.   8 in.

x

2.

32 in.

y y

x
Perimeter = 94 in.

Do you UNDERSTAND?

3. A sandbox is shaped like a rectangle. Its area is 48 square feet. The side lengths are whole numbers. What are possible dimensions of this sandbox? Do all possible dimensions make sense? Explain.

4. The length of a garden is 25 feet. What must the width of the garden be, in a whole number of feet, so the area is greater than 200 square feet but less than 300 square feet?

Independent Practice

MATHEMATICAL PRACTICES

© **Model** Find the missing dimension or dimensions.

5.

Area = 60 sq ft   6 ft

x

6.

x

y 5 in.

Perimeter = 30 in.

7.

22 yd

y

x
Perimeter = 84 yd

8.

x

Area = 81 sq mi   9 mi

Animated Glossary
www.pearsonsuccessnet.com

DIGITAL

50

Answer the hidden question.

Area = length × width

Think I know only the width. The hidden question is, "What is the length of the park?" I can use what I know to find the length.

7 + 7 = 14   Add the two known sides, since opposite sides of a rectangle are equal.

36 − 14 = 22   Subtract the total of the two known sides from the perimeter to find the total of the two unknown sides.

22 ÷ 2 = 11   Divide to find the length of one side.

The length of the park is 11 miles.

Use the answer to the hidden question to answer the original question.

ℓ = 11 miles

w = 7 miles

$A = \ell \times w$

$= 11 \times 7$

$= 77$

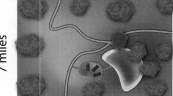

7 miles

11 miles

The area of the park is 77 square miles.

Problem Solving

MATHEMATICAL
PRACTICES

9. Mr. Chen is putting tile down in his kitchen. The kitchen is 16 feet long and 8 feet wide. The tile costs $5 per square foot. How much will it cost Mr. Chen to tile his kitchen?

10. Greg built a picture frame with a perimeter of 50 inches. It is 14 inches long. How wide is it?

Ⓒ 11. **Model** Julie planted a rectangular garden that is 20 feet long. She placed 56 feet of fencing around her garden. Draw and label a sketch of her garden. What is the width of her garden? What is the area?

12. Central Park in New York City has a length of $2\frac{1}{2}$ miles and a width of $\frac{1}{2}$ mile. What is the perimeter of the park?

 A $6\frac{1}{2}$ miles   **C** $5\frac{1}{2}$ miles

 B 6 miles   **D** $4\frac{1}{2}$ miles

Ⓒ 13. **Reason** Nancy wove a pot holder with an area of 80 square inches. The lengths and widths of the sides are whole numbers. Which dimensions make the most sense for a potholder? Explain.

14. The Green Darner is one of the largest dragonflies. It weighs about four hundredths of an ounce. Write four hundredths in standard form.

Ⓒ 15. **Persevere** An art class is planning to paint a rectangular mural with an area of 60 square feet. It has to be at least 4 feet high but no more than 6 feet high. How long could it be if the length and width have to be whole numbers?

Lesson
16-12A
ⓒ
Common Core

4.MD.2 Use the four operations to solve word problems involving distances, intervals of time, liquid volumes, masses of objects, and money, including problems involving simple fractions or decimals, and problems that require expressing measurements given in a larger unit in terms of a smaller unit. Represent measurement quantities using diagrams such as number line diagrams that feature a measurement scale.

Solving Measurement Problems

How can you use diagrams to solve measurement problems?

Andy is using a roll of fabric to make a sofa cushion like the one at the right. What is the total length of fabric Andy needs to make the cushion?

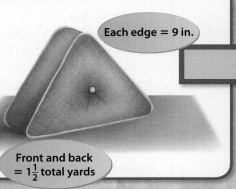

Each edge = 9 in.

Front and back = $1\frac{1}{2}$ total yards

Another Example

A runner finished a race in 2 hours 32 minutes. A walker finished the same race in 5 hours 8 minutes. How much faster was the runner's time than the walker's time? Use a bar diagram to compare the quantities and choose the operation.

x = 5 h 8 min − 2 h 32 min

= 4 h 68 min − 2 h 32 min

= 2 h 36 min

The runner finished 2 hours 36 minutes faster than the walker.

 **Tip** *1 hour = 60 minutes*

Walk	5 h 8 min	
Run	2 h 32 min	x

Guided Practice

ⓒ **MATHEMATICAL PRACTICES**

Do you know HOW?

Draw a bar diagram to help solve the problem.

1. A recipe for fruit punch is shown below. How much punch does the recipe make?

   FRUIT PUNCH

   $2\frac{1}{2}$ gallons orange juice
   3 quarts cranberry juice
   2 quarts apple juice

Do you UNDERSTAND?

ⓒ **2. Reason** In the example above, what fraction of a yard is 9 inches? How can fractions be used to find the total number of yards needed to make one of the sofa cushions?

3. A small sofa has a mass of 30 kilograms. A pillow on the sofa has a mass of 300 grams. How many pillows would it take to equal the mass of the sofa?

Draw a diagram to show the data. Change to common units.

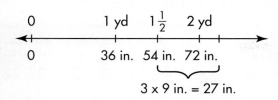

0   1 yd $1\frac{1}{2}$ 2 yd

0   36 in.   54 in.   72 in.

3 × 9 in. = 27 in.

 1 yard = 36 inches

Use the given data to solve the problem.

$1\frac{1}{2}$ yards = 54 inches

3 sides × 9 inches = 27 inches

54 in. + 27 in. = 81 in.

1 yd = 36 in.   2 yd = 72 in.

81 in. − 72 in. = 9 in.

So, 81 inches = 2 yards 9 inches

81 inches or 2 yards 9 inches of material are needed for the cushion.

Independent Practice

Use the diagram to help solve each problem.

4. A water jug has a capacity of $3\frac{1}{2}$ gallons. How many times will the coach have to fill a 2-cup measuring cup to fill the water jug?

1 c																

(table: rows labeled 1 gal, 1 qt, 1 pt, 1 c)

5. Geneva cut $1\frac{1}{4}$ yards from a spool of ribbon. Then she cut two 27-inch pieces of ribbon from the spool. How many inches of ribbon in all did Geneva cut from the spool? How many yards of ribbon did she cut?

0   1 yd   2 yd   3 yd

0   9 in.   18 in.   27 in.   36 in.

Problem Solving

MATHEMATICAL PRACTICES

© **6. Reason** The trail to a waterfall is $2\frac{1}{3}$ miles long. Signs are placed at the beginning and the end of the trail. There are also signs placed at each $\frac{1}{3}$ mile mark along the trail. How many signs are there on the trail?

© **7. Model** Mrs. Reed collects rocks. Each rock in her collection weighs about 4 ounces. Her collection weighs about 12 pounds in all. About how many rocks are in her collection?

A 3 rocks   **C** 36 rocks

B 4 rocks   **D** 48 rocks

Lesson
17-4A
Ⓒ
Common Core

4.MD.4 Make a line plot to display a data set of measurements in fractions of a unit ($\frac{1}{2}$, $\frac{1}{4}$, $\frac{1}{8}$). Solve problems involving addition and subtraction of fractions by using information presented in line plots.

Solving Problems Involving Line Plots

How can you use line plots to solve problems?

The results of a catch-and-release salmon fishing contest are shown in the chart at the right. What length of fish was caught most often? What is the difference between the longest and shortest lengths?

Fish Lengths, in inches

$24\frac{1}{2}$, $25\frac{3}{4}$, $26\frac{1}{4}$, $25\frac{1}{4}$, 23, $22\frac{3}{4}$,

$22\frac{3}{4}$, $21\frac{1}{4}$, $25\frac{1}{4}$, $25\frac{1}{4}$, $24\frac{1}{2}$, $22\frac{3}{4}$,

$22\frac{1}{4}$, $27\frac{1}{2}$, $25\frac{1}{4}$, $24\frac{1}{2}$, $22\frac{1}{4}$,

$22\frac{3}{4}$, $25\frac{1}{4}$, $27\frac{1}{2}$

Guided Practice

MATHEMATICAL PRACTICES

Do you know HOW?

For **1** and **2**, use the line plot showing results to a survey question.

Number of Cell Phone Calls Made Today

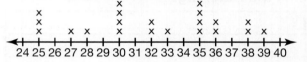

1. What was the greatest number of cell phone calls made?

2. What is the difference between the greatest and least number of calls?

Do you UNDERSTAND?

For **3–4**, use the data set below.

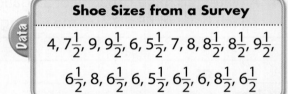

Shoe Sizes from a Survey

4, $7\frac{1}{2}$, 9, $9\frac{1}{2}$, 6, $5\frac{1}{2}$, 7, 8, $8\frac{1}{2}$, $8\frac{1}{2}$, $9\frac{1}{2}$,

$6\frac{1}{2}$, 8, $6\frac{1}{2}$, 6, $5\frac{1}{2}$, $6\frac{1}{2}$, 6, $8\frac{1}{2}$, $6\frac{1}{2}$

3. Make a line plot of the data.

Ⓒ **4. Use Tools** What is the most common shoe size?

Independent Practice

MATHEMATICAL PRACTICES

For **5** and **6**, use the line plot below.

Heights in inches of Dr. Chen's Patients

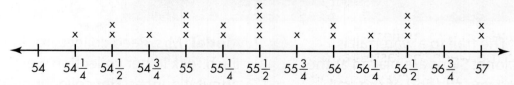

5. What is the difference between the tallest height and the shortest height?

Ⓒ **6. Critique Reasoning** Oscar says that 55 inches is the most common height Dr. Chen measured. Do you agree? Explain.

Animated Glossary
www.pearsonsuccessnet.com

Make line plots to show the data.

Remember a line plot <u>shows data along a number line.</u>

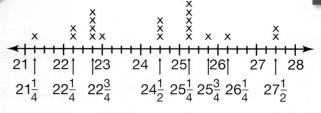

Fish Length—Catch-and-Release Salmon Contest

Use the line plot to solve the problems.

The most Xs are for $25\frac{1}{4}$ in. This is the length of fish caught most often.

Longest fish: $27\frac{2}{4}$ in.

Shortest fish: $21\frac{1}{4}$ in.

$$27\frac{1}{2} - 21\frac{1}{4} = 27\frac{2}{4} - 21\frac{1}{4} = 6\frac{1}{4}$$

The difference between the longest fish and the shortest fish was $6\frac{1}{4}$ in.

Problem Solving

For **7** through **9,** use the line plot on the right.

© **7. Reason** How many students are in Mrs. Harper's class? Explain how you found your answer.

Number of Pets Each Student Has

8. How many students have 3 pets? How many pets in all is that?

9. What is the total number of pets the students in Mrs. Harper's class have?

   A 25   **C** 42

   B 34   **D** 52

For **10** through **12,** use the results of the men's and women's races, shown on the right.

© **10. Use Tools** Make a line plot of each set of times.

11. Which race had the smallest difference between the fastest and slowest times? Show how you found your answer.

12. Using the line plots you made, what can you tell about how the runners in each race were grouped when they crossed the finish line?

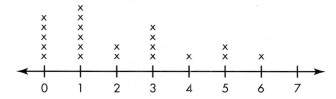

Men's Times (seconds)	10.38, 10.32, 10.31, 10.41, 10.41, 10.25, 10.41, 10.38, 10.38, 10.32, 10.38, 10.41, 10.32, 10.38, 10.38
Women's Times (seconds)	10.45, 10.31, 10.32, 10.37, 10.32, 10.32, 10.36, 10.32, 10.37, 10.41, 10.31, 10.31, 10.45, 10.31, 10.32